# 100+ Science Experiments for School and Home

**Editors:** Mary Dieterich and Sarah M. Anderson
**Consultant:** Schyrlet Cameron
**Proofreader:** Margaret Brown

COPYRIGHT © 2012 Mark Twain Media, Inc.

ISBN 978-1-58037-618-1

Printing No. CD-404163

Mark Twain Media, Inc., Publishers
Distributed by Carson-Dellosa Publishing LLC

**Visit us at www.carsondellosa.com**

# Table of Contents

# Table of Contents (cont.)

# Table of Contents (cont.)

# Table of Contents (cont.)

# Introduction

The world of information is expanding at such an unbelievable rate due to technology. Satellites allow instant communication between every nook and cranny throughout the world. Television coverage can be instantaneous, and computers, through the Internet, give access to millions of pieces of information, covering every conceivable subject.

Students living in this exploding age of technology are fortunate that so much is available to them. However, sometimes the glut of information can completely overwhelm students, causing them to throw up their hands and become discouraged. This is where the teacher can help the learner focus on the basics.

This science experiments book is designed to enable the student to focus on basic science principles that seem obvious to some students but are elusive to others. A structured approach to learning these principles is important to each individual.

Students need to develop the habit of looking at the world around them, using an organized approach to learning. This will serve them well throughout their lives.

# How to Use This Book

It is suggested that students develop the habit of looking at "things" in the world using a form of the "scientific method." We suggest that the students use the following steps to organize their experiments/demonstrations/projects. This is just one of the many forms of the scientific method. Possible steps are as follows:

1. Ask a question.
2. Review what is known about the topic.
3. Formulate a hypothesis.
4. Experiment to test the hypothesis.
5. Observe the experiment; record and organize the results.
6. Analyze the results and draw conclusions.
7. Share the results with others.

Each activity may be completed as an individual student experiment, demonstration, or project, or activities may be completed by student teams. Activities may also be done as whole-class experiments, demonstrations, or projects. Some of the activities might be best done by teacher demonstration. Choice of method many times will depend on lab facilities, availability of equipment and supplies, time, and most importantly, student safety.

Regardless of whether the activity is conducted as an experiment or demonstration, the students will need to follow the steps of an identified scientific method. We have provided a suggested method above that may be modified to fit your classroom needs.

It is suggested that you duplicate and make readily available to your students a supply of the sample and blank Experiment/Demonstration Forms found on pages x–xiv of this book. Students may then add the completed Experiment/Demonstration Forms to their ongoing science journals.

# National Science Standards Matrix

Each unit of study is designed to strengthen scientific literacy skills and support the National Science Education Standards (NSES).

| Experiment/Demonstration | Content Standards* | | | | | | | |
| --- | --- | --- | --- | --- | --- | --- | --- | --- |
| **Weather** | Unifying Concepts and Processes | A | B | C | D | E | F | G |
| How Do We Know That Air Exerts Pressure? | X | X | X | | X | | | |
| What Are Some of the Uses of Air Pressure? | X | X | X | | X | | | |
| How Can We Make a Simple Barometer? | X | X | X | | X | | | |
| How Is a Barometer Used? | X | X | X | | X | | | |
| How Do Heating and Cooling Affect a Solid? | X | X | X | | X | | | |
| What Happens to a Bimetallic Strip When It Is Heated? | X | X | X | | X | | | |
| How Can We Demonstrate the Principle of the Thermostat? | X | X | X | | X | | | |
| How Can We Make a Bimetallic Strip? | X | X | X | | X | | | |
| What Are Some of the Effects of Cooling and Heating Liquid? | X | X | X | | X | | | |
| What Are Some of the Effects of Cooling and Heating Air? | X | X | X | | X | | | |
| How is Heat Transferred by Radiation? | X | X | X | | X | | | |
| How Can We Demonstrate Convection Currents in a Liquid? | X | X | X | | X | | | |
| How Can We Demonstrate Convection Currents (Wind) in Air? | X | X | X | | X | | | |
| How Can We Make a Simple Thermometer? | X | X | X | | X | | | |
| How Can We Make a Simple Weather Vane? | X | X | | | X | | | |
| How Can We Make a Simple Anemometer? | X | X | | | X | | | |
| What Effect Does Water Have on Weather Conditions? | X | X | X | | X | | | |
| What Are Some Reasons for Changes in the Rate of Evaporation? | X | X | X | | X | | | |
| Do Some Solids Evaporate Directly From a Solid to a Gas? | X | X | X | | X | | | |
| What Effect Does Evaporation Have on Temperature? | X | X | X | | X | | | |
| What Do We Mean by Relative Humidity? | X | X | X | | X | | | |
| How Can We Determine the Dew Point of the Air? | X | X | X | | X | | | |
| How Can We Demonstrate Cloud Forms? | X | X | | | X | | | |
| How Can We Make a Cloud? | X | X | | | X | | | |
| What Is the Water Cycle? | X | X | | X | X | | | |
| How Can We Make a Hygrometer? | X | X | X | X | X | | | |
| How Can We Make Smog? | X | X | | X | | | | |
| What Is Sleet? | X | X | | X | | | | |

# National Science Standards Matrix (cont.)

| Experiment/Demonstration | Content Standards* | | | | | | | |
|---|---|---|---|---|---|---|---|---|
| **Water** | Unifying Concepts and Processes | A | B | C | D | E | F | G |
| Does Water Exert Pressure? | x | x | x | | | | | |
| What Is the Water Table? | x | x | | | x | | | |
| What Is the Effect of Lowering the Water Table? | x | x | | | x | | | |
| Upon What Does the Height of the Water Table Depend? | x | x | | | x | | | |
| What Is the Effect of the Water Table on Seedlings? | x | x | | x | x | | | |
| How Can We Chemically Remove Impurities From Water? | x | x | x | | | | | |
| How Can We Filter Water? | x | x | x | | x | | | |
| How Can We Distill Water? | x | x | x | | x | | | |
| What Is the Function of Soap? | x | x | x | | | | | |
| What Is The Disadvantage of Hard Water? | x | x | x | | x | | | |
| How Can We Make Water Softer? | x | x | x | | x | | | |
| **Airplanes, Jets, and Rockets** | | | | | | | | |
| How Does Changing Air Pressure Affect Objects? | x | x | x | | | | | |
| How Is a Plane Lifted? | x | x | x | | | | | |
| How Is Thrust Provided by Propellers? | x | x | x | | | | | |
| How Is Lift Provided by an Airplane? | x | x | x | | | | | |
| How Can We Demonstrate Drag? | x | x | x | | | | | |
| How Can We Demonstrate Thrust in Jets and Rockets? | x | x | x | | | | | |
| How Can We Demonstrate the Principle of the Helicopter? | x | x | x | | | | | |
| How Can We Demonstrate the Function of Elevators and Rudders? | x | x | x | | | | | |
| How Can We Demonstrate the Function of the Ailerons? | x | x | x | | | | | |
| Air Safety: For What Are Seat Belts Used? | x | x | x | | | | | |
| How Can We Make a Parachute? | x | x | x | | | | | |
| What Is the Principle of Artificial Satellites? What is Meant by Centrifugal Force? | x | x | x | | x | | | |
| **Time and Place** | | | | | | | | |
| How Should We Approach the Study of Time? | x | x | | | x | | | |
| What Are Some Devices for Keeping Time? | x | x | | x | x | | | |
| Upon What Does the Period of a Pendulum Depend? | x | x | | x | x | | | |
| What Are the Time Zones in the United States? | x | x | | x | x | | | |
| How Can We Make a Time Cone? | x | x | | x | x | | | |
| How Can We Use a Sextant to Measure Latitude? | x | x | | x | x | | | |
| How Can We Make a Sextant? | x | x | | x | x | | | |

# National Science Standards Matrix (cont.)

| Experiment/Demonstration | Content Standards* | | | | | | | |
|---|---|---|---|---|---|---|---|---|
| **The Earth's Surface** | Unifying Concepts and Processes | A | B | C | D | E | F | G |
| How Can We Collect and Study Rocks? | x | x | | | x | | | |
| How Can Rock Collections Be Made? | x | x | | | x | | | |
| What Is the Test for Limestone? | x | x | x | | x | | | |
| What Do Crystals Look Like? | x | x | | | x | | | |
| What Are the Effects of Water on Rocks? | x | x | | | x | | | |
| How Are New Rocks Formed? | x | x | | | x | | | |
| How Are Fossils Formed? | x | x | | | x | | | |
| What Effects Do Plants Have on Rocks? | x | x | | x | x | | | |
| How Does Water Wear Away the Earth's Surface in Some Places and Build it Up in Others? | x | x | | | x | | | |
| How Can We Demonstrate the Formation of Stalactites and Stalagmites in Caves? | x | x | | | x | | | |
| What Determines How Big Crystals Will Get? | x | x | | | x | | | |
| How Can We Demonstrate Some of the Geological Features Formed by a Stream? | x | x | | | x | | | |
| How Can We Demonstrate the Action of Ice in Changing the Earth's Surface? | x | x | x | | x | | | |
| How Do We Know That Ice Contains Particles? | x | x | | | x | | | |
| How Are Kettle Holes Formed? | x | x | | | x | | | |
| Does Air Carry Sediments? | x | x | | | x | | | |
| How Are Sand Dunes Formed? | x | x | | | x | | | |
| What Are the Forces That Help Make Soil? | x | x | | | x | | | |
| What Are the Constituencies of Soil? | x | x | | | x | | | |
| How Is Soil Tested? | x | x | x | | x | | | |
| How Can We Demonstrate Soil Erosion and Conservation? | x | x | | x | x | | | |
| How Is the Earth's Surface Built Up? | x | x | | | x | | | |
| How Can We Show a Cause for Faulting? | x | x | | | x | | | |
| What Is the Cause of Unequal Heating of the Land? | x | x | | | x | | | |
| Is Water a Poor Conductor of Heat? | x | x | x | | x | | | |
| How Many Inches of Snow Equal One Inch of Rain? | x | x | x | | x | | | |
| How Can We Demonstrate Dew? | x | x | | | x | | | |
| How Can We Make Frost? | x | x | | | x | | | |
| How Can We Make a Simple Rain Gauge? | x | x | | | x | | | |

*For more detailed information on each content standard, visit < www.nap.edu/catalog/4962.html> or see the book *National Science Education Standards* (ISBN 0-309-05326-9).

## Sample Experiment/Demonstration Form

## Question:

How can we prove that air exerts pressure?

## Review what is known about the question:

Obtain information about this topic in the library and on the Internet.

## Formulate a hypothesis:

"Air pressure is due to the weight of the air above us."

## Experiment/Demonstration to test your hypothesis:

**Step 1:** Place a hard-boiled egg (shell removed) on the opening of an empty glass orange-juice bottle or fruit-juice bottle with the opening in the bottle approximately 1 1/2 inches in diameter. What happens? (Record observations.)

*The egg cannot be pushed through the opening of the bottle without exerting force.*

**Step 2:** Remove the egg and insert a flaming torch made from a piece of rolled-up paper into the bottle. What happens? (Record observations.)

*The paper burns in the bottle.*

**Step 3:** Quickly replace the egg on top of the bottle. What happens? (Record observations.)

*The paper burns until the oxygen in the bottle is used up and the egg is sucked into the jar.*

## Sample Experiment/Demonstration Form (cont.)

**Step 4:** _____
_____
_____

**Repeat the experiment if necessary for further data:**

_____
_____
_____
_____
_____
_____
_____
_____
_____

**Analyze results and draw conclusions:**

The flame uses up most of the oxygen in the bottle. Since there is less pressure pushing upward and more pressure pushing downward, the egg is literally "pushed" into the
bottle. This demonstrates that the air outside the bottle does exert pressure.

_____

**Share the results with others and add this information to your science journal.**

# Experiment/Demonstration # _____

**Question:**

_____

_____

_____

_____

**Review what is known about the question:**

_____

_____

_____

_____

_____

_____

**Formulate a hypothesis:**

_____

_____

_____

**Experiment/Demonstration to test your hypothesis:**

**Step 1:** _____

_____

_____

_____

**Experiment/Demonstration # _____ (cont.)**

**Step 2:** _____

_____

_____

_____

_____

**Step 3:** _____

_____

_____

_____

_____

**Step 4:** _____

_____

_____

_____

_____

**Repeat the experiment if necessary for further data:**

_____

_____

_____

_____

_____

_____

_____

## Experiment/Demonstration # _____ (cont.)

**Analyze results and draw conclusions:**

_____

_____

_____

_____

_____

_____

_____

_____

_____

_____

_____

_____

_____

_____

_____

_____

_____

_____

_____

_____

**Share the results with others and add this information to your science journal.**

# How Do We Know That Air Exerts Pressure?

## EXPERIMENT/DEMONSTRATION #1

### MATERIALS NEEDED:

Hard-boiled egg
Matches or lighter
Orange-juice bottle or fruit-juice bottle
Rolled-up sheet of paper
*Adult supervision and the use of safety goggles
are recommended.*

### PROCEDURE:

**Step 1:** Place a hard-boiled egg (shell removed) on top of an empty orange-juice bottle or fruit-juice bottle with an opening in the bottle approximately 1 1/2 inches in diameter. The egg cannot be pushed through the opening of the bottle.

**Step 2:** Remove the egg and insert a flaming torch made from a piece of rolled-up paper into the bottle.

**Step 3:** Quickly replace the egg on top of the bottle.

**What happens?** _____

_____

_____

_____

# How Do We Know That Air Exerts Pressure? (cont.)

## EXPERIMENT/DEMONSTRATION #2

**MATERIALS NEEDED:**

One-gallon rectangular metal can with cap
Vacuum pump

**PROCEDURE:**

**Step 1:** Obtain a discarded rectangular gallon metal can with a cap (varnish, wax, or syrup can). Make sure the can is clean.

**Step 2:** Pump out the air with a vacuum pump.

**What happens?** (Use the form at the beginning of this book or your own paper.)

## EXPERIMENT/DEMONSTRATION #3

**MATERIALS NEEDED:**

Deep dish or jar          Water          Clear tumbler

**PROCEDURE:**

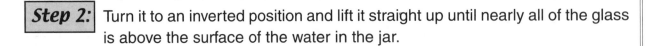

**Step 1:** In a deep dish or jar full of water, submerge a clear tumbler and allow it to fill with water.

**Step 2:** Turn it to an inverted position and lift it straight up until nearly all of the glass is above the surface of the water in the jar.

**What happens?** (Use the form at the beginning of this book or your own paper.)

## How Do We Know That Air Exerts Pressure? (cont.)

### EXPERIMENT/DEMONSTRATION #4

#### MATERIALS NEEDED:

One-gallon rectangular metal can with cap

Water

Hot pads or oven mitts

Hot plate or Bunsen burner

*Adult supervision and the use of safety goggles*
*and hot pads are recommended.*

#### PROCEDURE:

**Step 1:** Obtain a discarded rectangular gallon metal can with a cap, and make sure it is rinsed out. Put a small amount of water into the can.

**Step 2:** Heat the water with a hot plate or Bunsen burner.

**Step 3:** Using hot pads or oven mitts, quickly remove the can from the heat and put the cap tightly on the opening of the can. Set the can aside and watch it.

**What happens?** _____

_____

_____

# How Do We Know That Air Exerts Pressure? (cont.)

## EXPERIMENT/DEMONSTRATION #5

### MATERIALS NEEDED:

Drinking glass

Water

Playing card

Pail or similar container

*Caution: Perform this experiment over a pail or similar container.*

### PROCEDURE:

**Step 1:** Fill a glass to the top with water.

**Step 2:** On the top of the glass, place a card that is larger than the diameter of the glass.

**Step 3:** Holding the card firmly on the glass, quickly turn the glass over.

**Step 4:** Remove your hand from the card carefully.

**What happens?** _____

_____

_____

_____

# How Do We Know That Air Exerts Pressure? (cont.)

## EXPERIMENT/DEMONSTRATION #6

### MATERIALS NEEDED:

Small tin can (soup can)          Nail

Water                                      Hammer

*Adult supervision and the use of safety goggles are recommended.*

### PROCEDURE:

**Step 1:** Using a hammer, make a nail hole near the bottom of a small tin can.

**Step 2:** Fill the can with water.

**Step 3:** Hold the palm of your hand tightly over the top of the can.

**What happens?** _____

_____

_____

**Step 4:** Lift your hand.

**What happens?** _____

_____

_____

# What Are Some of the Uses of Air Pressure?

## EXPERIMENT/DEMONSTRATION #7

**MATERIALS NEEDED:**

Empty soda bottle          Drinking straw
Clay                       Water

**PROCEDURE:**

**Step 1:** Fill a soda bottle with water.

**Step 2:** Place a drinking straw in the soda bottle full of water.

**Step 3:** Press clay around the straw and the bottle.

**Step 4:** Hold the clay tightly to the bottle with your fingers and try to drink through the straw.

**What happens?** _____

_____

_____

_____

# What Are Some of the Uses of Air Pressure? (cont.)

## EXPERIMENT/DEMONSTRATION #8

### MATERIALS NEEDED:

Glass tube　　　　Empty soda bottle
One-hole stopper　　Water

### PROCEDURE:

**Step 1:** Fill a soda bottle completely with water.

**Step 2:** Insert a glass tube into a one-hole stopper.

**Step 3:** Insert the stopper into the filled soda bottle.

**Step 4:** Suck on the tube and try to get a drink of water.

**Step 5:** Loosen the stopper and try to take another drink of water.

**What happens?** _____

_____

_____

_____

# What Are Some of the Uses of Air Pressure? (cont.)

## EXPERIMENT/DEMONSTRATION #9

### MATERIALS NEEDED:

Glass jar
Empty dish or pan (like a pie pan)
Water
Clay
Eyedropper

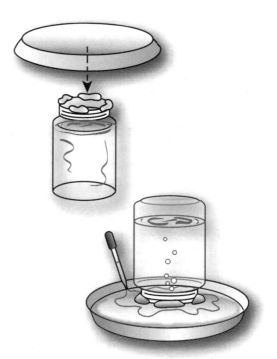

### PROCEDURE:

**Step 1:** Press four or five lumps of clay over the rim of a glass jar.

**Step 2:** Fill the jar with water.

**Step 3:** Set a dish or pan in an inverted position on the lumps of clay.

**Step 4:** Now, with one hand on the dish or pan and the other holding the jar, quickly invert both the dish and the jar.

**Step 5:** Use the eyedropper to remove some of the water in the dish.

**Step 6:** Watch for air bubbles to enter the jar as water is removed.

Bottles of drinking water are often inverted in this way in office buildings.

# How Can We Make a Simple Barometer?

## EXPERIMENT/DEMONSTRATION #10

### MATERIALS NEEDED:

Shallow jar or can
String or rubber bands
Thin sheet of rubber (size depends on size of jar or can)
Glue (that will hold plastic to rubber)
Drinking straw
Wood splint (toothpick or match)
Cardboard (calibrated to "high" and "low")
Small block of wood (or something to keep cardboard upright)

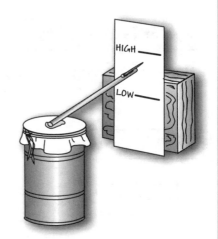

### PROCEDURE:

**Step 1:** Stretch a piece of thin rubber over the mouth of a shallow can or jar.

**Step 2:** Tie string tightly around the top of the can or jar to hold the rubber piece in place.

**Step 3:** Glue a drinking straw on the piece of rubber so one end of the straw is on the center of the rubber.

**Step 4:** Fasten a small piece of toothpick or match to the other end of the straw to act as a pointer.

**Step 5:** Place the can or jar so the pointer is not quite touching a piece of paper or cardboard that has been calibrated as "high" and "low."

**What happens?** _____

_____

_____

**Step 6:** Record your readings daily and discuss the operational principle of this improvised barometer.

# How Can We Make a Simple Barometer? (cont.)

## EXPERIMENT/DEMONSTRATION #11

### MATERIALS NEEDED:

Bent glass tubing     Food coloring
Water                 Thermos bottle

### PROCEDURE:

**Step 1:** Make a thermos-bottle barometer as shown in the diagram at right.

**Step 2:** Add a few drops of food coloring to water and pour it into the bent glass tubing. Note the effect on the liquid as the pressure changes from day to day.

**Step 3:** Discuss the reason for using a thermos bottle rather than an uninsulated bottle. Discuss the limitations of this type of barometer.

**Step 4:** Variations in atmospheric pressure are the least noticeable of the changes in air conditions. Collect evidence of the changes in atmospheric pressure that accompany weather changes.

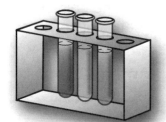

# How Is a Barometer Used?

---

## EXPERIMENT/DEMONSTRATION #12

### MATERIALS NEEDED:

The barometers made in previous experiments:
- simple barometer
- thermos-bottle barometer

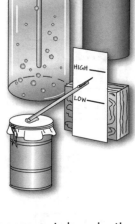

### PROCEDURE:

If there are differences in elevation on or near the school grounds, it will be interesting to take barometric readings at the highest and lowest points.

It is also interesting to take a barometer along on a field trip. It may be possible to encounter multiple barometric readings throughout the trip, especially if the trip involves climbing hills.

A finely calibrated barometer will show a difference when readings are taken in the basement and on the top floor of the school building.

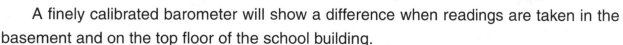

**Step 1:** Record the reading of the barometer in each place for several days. Make a graph of the daily pressure changes over that same period to relate the pressure changes to weather changes.

**Step 2:** After keeping barometric pressure readings for several days, an understanding of the reasons for the variations should develop. Point out that there are great waves in the atmosphere just as there are waves in the ocean. There are also great air currents similar in some ways to ocean currents.

# How Do Heating and Cooling Affect a Solid?

## EXPERIMENT/DEMONSTRATION #13

### MATERIALS NEEDED:

Small weight                    Length of copper wire
Support for wire and weight     Candle or Bunsen burner
*Adult supervision and the use of safety goggles are recommended.*

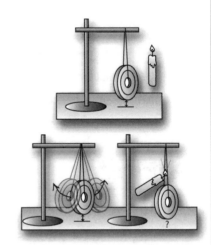

### PROCEDURE:

**Step 1:** Tie a weight to a length of copper wire.

**Step 2:** Hang the wire from a support and allow it to swing freely, approximately 1/16 of an inch above a table top.

**Step 3:** Swing the weight back and forth, and then heat the wire with a candle or burner. Eventually the weight will touch the table and stop swinging. If the wire is allowed to cool, the weight will swing freely again.

**Why?** _____

_____

_____

_____

# How Do Heating and Cooling Affect a Solid? (cont.)

## EXPERIMENT/DEMONSTRATION #14

### MATERIALS NEEDED:

Two supports      Two lengths of copper wire
Ruler             Small weight
Candle or Bunsen burner
*Adult supervision and the use of safety goggles are recommended.*

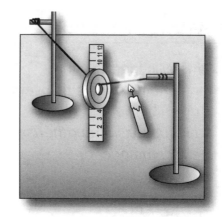

### PROCEDURE:

**Step 1:** Suspend a length of copper wire horizontally between two supports.

**Step 2:** Hang a weight from the middle of the wire.

**Step 3:** Measure the distance from the end of the weight to the table top.

**Step 4:** Heat the horizontal copper wire with a candle or Bunsen burner.

**Step 5:** Now measure the distance from the end of the weight to the table top.

**What happens?** _____

_____

_____

**Why?** _____

_____

_____

As a variation, try using different types of metal wire and make a graph of your findings.

# What Happens to a Bimetallic Strip When It Is Heated?

## EXPERIMENT/DEMONSTRATION #15

### MATERIALS NEEDED:

Bimetallic thermal strip
Tongs (to hold the strip over the flame)
Bunsen burner
*Adult supervision and the use of safety goggles are recommended.*

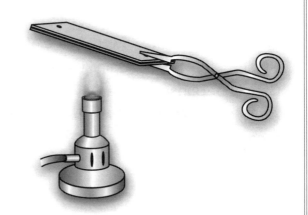

### PROCEDURE:

Obtain a bimetallic thermal strip consisting of a strip of brass and another of steel riveted closely together. Using the tongs, hold the strip over the Bunsen burner.

**What happens when the strip is heated?** _____

_____

_____

_____

_____

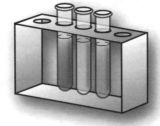

# How Can We Demonstrate the Principle of the Thermostat?

## EXPERIMENT/DEMONSTRATION #16

### MATERIALS NEEDED:

Bimetallic strip          Small lamp
Batteries                 Wire
Ring stand                Candle
*Adult supervision and the use of safety goggles are recommended.*

### PROCEDURE:

**Step 1:** Clamp a bimetallic strip in a horizontal position to a support.

**Step 2:** Attach a wire to the bimetallic strip and place it in a circuit with batteries and a small lamp.

**Step 3:** Attach the end of a wire leading from the lamp to another support so it touches the end of the bimetallic strip.

**Step 4:** Heat the strip with a candle. This causes it to bend upward and break the circuit. As soon as the strip cools, it bends downward again and completes the circuit. The lamp represents the motors that drive a furnace and circulators.

# How Can We Make a Bimetallic Strip?

## EXPERIMENT/DEMONSTRATION #17

### MATERIALS NEEDED:

Tin can
Tin snips
Candle or Bunsen burner
Bare copper wire
Clamp
*Adult supervision and the use of safety goggles and gloves are recommended.*
<u>Caution</u>: *Clamp one end of the metal in position to prevent burns.*

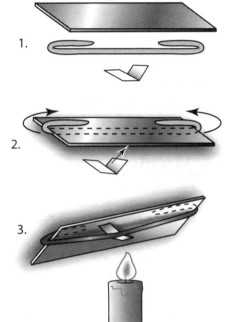

### PROCEDURE:

**Step 1:** Cut a strip of tin from a can with the tin snips and loop the ends of a bare copper wire over the ends of the strip of tin as shown in the diagram.

**Step 2:** Stretch the wire by inserting a shorter strip of metal bent into a V-shape.

**Step 3:** Heat.

**What happens?** _____

_____

_____

_____

_____

# What Are Some of the Effects of Cooling and Heating Liquid?

## EXPERIMENT/DEMONSTRATION #18

### MATERIALS NEEDED:

Flask
One-hole stopper
Water
Food coloring
Long glass tube

### PROCEDURE:

**Step 1:** Put some colored water into a flask.

**Step 2:** Insert a long glass tube through a one-hole stopper to the bottom of the flask. The level of liquid can be adjusted by blowing in a bubble or releasing the stopper to let some air out.

**Step 3:** Warm and cool the flask.

**What happens?** _____

_____

_____

_____

# What Are Some of the Effects of Cooling and Heating Air?

## EXPERIMENT/DEMONSTRATION #19

### MATERIALS NEEDED:

Two large flasks            String
Support                     Yard or meter stick
Bunsen burner
*Adult supervision and the use of safety goggles are recommended.*

### PROCEDURE:

**Step 1:** Tie lengths of string around the necks of two large flasks.

**Step 2:** Suspend the flasks from each end of a yard or meter stick.

**Step 3:** Suspend the center of the stick from a support as shown above and balance the two flasks.

**Step 4:** Heat one of the flasks with the Bunsen burner.

**What happens?** _____

_____

_____

_____

# What Are Some of the Effects of Cooling and Heating Air? (cont.)

## EXPERIMENT/DEMONSTRATION #20

### MATERIALS NEEDED:

Large balloon
Large flask
Bunsen burner
Stand
*Adult supervision and the use of safety goggles are recommended.*

### PROCEDURE:

**Step 1:** Stretch a large, empty balloon over the mouth of a flask.

**Step 2:** Place the flask on a stand over the Bunsen burner and heat the flask.

**What happens?** _____

_____

_____

_____

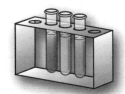

# How Is Heat Transferred by Radiation?

## EXPERIMENT/DEMONSTRATION #21

### MATERIALS NEEDED:

Two test tubes
Black marker or tape
Light source (or the sun)
Water
Thermometers

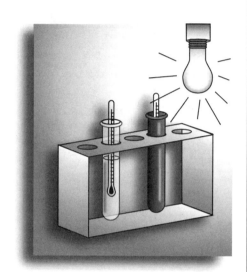

### PROCEDURE:

**Step 1:** Cover a test tube with black marker or black tape.

**Step 2:** Fill the black test tube with water.

**Step 3:** Fill a clear test tube with water.

**Step 4:** Insert a thermometer into each.

**Step 5:** Place both in a direct light source for 30 minutes.

*What happens to the temperature in each test tube?*

_____

_____

_____

_____

## How Can We Demonstrate Convection Currents in a Liquid?

### EXPERIMENT/DEMONSTRATION #22

**MATERIALS NEEDED:**

Bottle                     Two-hole stopper
Food coloring              Two glass tubes
Large beaker               Hot and cold water

**PROCEDURE:**

**Step 1:** Equip a bottle with a two-hole stopper.

**Step 2:** Extend a glass tube out of the bottle and another to reach close to the bottom of the bottle.

**Step 3:** Fill the bottle with hot water dyed with food coloring and place the stopper on the bottle.

**Step 4:** Submerge the bottle in a large beaker of cold water.

**What happens?** _____

_____

_____

_____

## How Can We Demonstrate Convection Currents (Wind) in Air?

### EXPERIMENT/DEMONSTRATION #23

**MATERIALS NEEDED:**

Paper or lightweight cardboard
Pencil
Scissors
String
Heat source (e.g., candle)
*Adult supervision and the use of safety goggles are recommended.*

**PROCEDURE:**

**Step 1:** Draw a spiral on a sheet of paper or lightweight cardboard, and, if desired, draw a snake's head at the outer end.

**Step 2:** Cut out the spiral and suspend it by a piece of string tied to the inner end over a source of heat.

**What happens?** _____

_____

_____

_____

_____

_____

_____

# How Can We Make a Simple Thermometer?

## EXPERIMENT/DEMONSTRATION #24

### MATERIALS NEEDED:

Flask                     One-hole stopper
Water                     Glass tube
Food coloring             Burner
Tape                      White card
A dish or pan of cold water
Classroom thermometer to show room temperature
*Adult supervision and the use of safety goggles are recommended.*

COLD WATER

### PROCEDURE:

Use the apparatus in the diagram to show how a thermometer works.

**Step 1:** Fill a flask with water and add food coloring.

**Step 2:** Insert the glass tube through the stopper and insert the stopper in the flask.

**Step 3:** Heat the flask over a burner or set it in the sunlight. Notice the rise in the water column in the tube.

**Step 4:** Tape the white card to the top of the tube.

**Step 5:** On the following day, when the water in the flask is the same temperature as the air in the classroom, make a mark on the white card taped to the tube at the water level in the tube. Opposite this mark, indicate the room temperature as indicated by the classroom thermometer.

# How Can We Make a Simple Thermometer? (cont.)

## EXPERIMENT/DEMONSTRATION #25

### MATERIALS NEEDED:

Flask                    Ring stand
Small beaker             Glass tube
One-hole stopper         Food coloring
Water

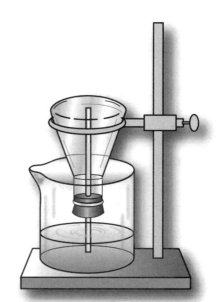

### PROCEDURE:

A simple air thermometer like the one in the diagram illustrates the relatively greater expansion and contraction of gases with changes in temperature as compared to liquids.

**Step 1:** Put food coloring in the water and pour the colored water into the small beaker.

**Step 2:** Insert the glass tube through the stopper, and then insert the stopper in the flask.

**Step 3:** Invert the flask with the glass tube into the beaker.

**Step 4:** Heat the flask gently with the palms of the hands to drive out air bubbles, and then let it cool.

**What happens?** _____

_____

_____

_____

# How Can We Make a Simple Weather Vane?

## EXPERIMENT/DEMONSTRATION #26

### MATERIALS NEEDED:

Wood or metal "arrow" and "feather"
Wooden base          Dowel rod or stick
Hammer and nail      Strip of wood
Drill                Glue
Black marker
*Adult supervision and the use of safety goggles are recommended.*

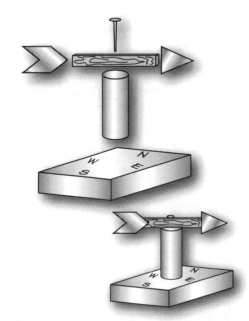

### PROCEDURE:

**Step 1:** Make a thin wood or metal "arrow" and "feather" as shown in the diagram.

**Step 2:** Fasten to a strip of wood.

**Step 3:** Balance the arrangement on a knife edge and drill a vertical hole at the place where it balances. Place a nail in the hole.

**Step 4:** Attach the arrow to the dowel rod by driving the nail vertically into the center of a dowel rod or the end of an upright stick, and mount the other end of the dowel rod or stick onto the center of the wooden base with glue.

**Step 5:** Indicate the directions N, S, E, and W on the base.

**Step 6:** Set the weather vane outside with the directions on the base facing actual north, etc. Do not place the weather vane too close to a building.

# How Can We Make a Simple Anemometer?

## EXPERIMENT/DEMONSTRATION #27

### MATERIALS NEEDED:

Four paper cups          Scissors
One small nail           Tape
Pencil                   One empty milk jug or carton
Black marker             Two 10 x 30-cm strips of cardboard
Sand                     One 45 x 4-cm strip of thin cardboard

### PROCEDURE:

**Step 1:** Cut a 10-cm slit in the side of each paper cup. Mark one paper cup with an "X" using a black marker.

**Step 2:** Find the center of each 10 x 30-cm strip of cardboard. Overlap the two strips to form a cross, matching the centers. Tape the two strips together.

**Step 3:** Slide each end of the crossed strips through the slit in one of the cups. (Be sure all cups face the same direction.)

**Step 4:** Carefully put a small nail through the center of the two strips.

**Step 5:** Roll the 45 x 4-cm strip of cardboard into a long tube no larger than one centimeter in diameter. Tape the tube so it stays rolled. Place one end of the tube in the empty milk jug or carton.

**Step 6:** Carefully add sand to the jug or carton until the tube is able to stand upright freely.

**Step 7:** Place the crossed strips of cardboard over the tube, putting the nail in the center of the tube.

**Step 8:** Set the anemometer outside and observe how many times the x-marked cup makes a complete spin around in one minute.

# What Effect Does Water Have on Weather Conditions?

## EXPERIMENT/DEMONSTRATION #28

### PROCEDURE:

Demonstrate in various ways that water is constantly evaporating into the air. Invert a jar over a potted plant, breathe on a window, or wash the chalkboard and watch the film of water disappear.

In discussing evaporation, it is interesting to note that when the relative humidity in an average-size classroom is 100%, the air will contain about 3,000 ml of water. Measure out 3 liters of water to demonstrate how much that is.

## EXPERIMENT/DEMONSTRATION #29

### MATERIALS NEEDED:

Piece of cloth      Two clothes hangers
Water               String
Long stick          Weight

### PROCEDURE:

**Step 1:** Dip a cloth in water. Wring out the cloth and place it on a hanger.

**Step 2:** Hook the clothes hanger on one end of a long stick.

**Step 3:** Balance the stick by attaching something on the other end of the stick that is of equal weight to the wet cloth.

### What happens as the water evaporates? _____

_____

_____

# *What Are Some Reasons for Changes in the Rate of Evaporation?*

## EXPERIMENT/DEMONSTRATION #30

### MATERIALS NEEDED:

Water
Graduated cylinder
Large container (e.g., large beaker)

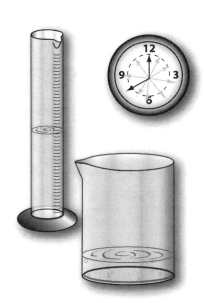

### PROCEDURE:

**Step 1:** Measure out 50 milliliters of water with a graduated cylinder and pour it into a vessel of much larger diameter.

**Step 2:** Again measure 50 milliliters in the graduated cylinder and allow it to remain in the cylinder.

**How much water has evaporated from each after 24 hours?**

_____

**Are the amounts different? Why?** _____

_____

_____

# Do Some Solids Evaporate
# Directly From a Solid to a Gas?

## EXPERIMENT/DEMONSTRATION #31

### MATERIALS NEEDED:

Dry ice          Spoon          Glass of water

*Adult supervision and the use of safety goggles and gloves are recommended.*

### PROCEDURE:

Expose a small piece of dry ice to the air until it disappears. Place another small piece in a glass of water and watch the escape of the bubbles of carbon dioxide. This is an example of the evaporation of solids, which is generally not as well known as the evaporation of liquids.

An interesting mechanical effect may be shown by placing the bowl of a spoon on a piece of dry ice with the spoon handle lying on the desk or table. A high-pitched sound will be noted as the gas escapes.

Camphor, mothballs, iodine crystals, and other substances will also evaporate. This is additional evidence that they are made up of tiny invisible particles in constant motion.

## What Effect Does Evaporation Have on Temperature?

## EXPERIMENT/DEMONSTRATION #32

### MATERIALS NEEDED:

Rubbing alcohol          Cotton ball or tissue
Someone's hand

### PROCEDURE:

Moisten the back of a hand with a little rubbing alcohol.

### What happens to the temperature of the hand?

_____

# What Do We Mean by Relative Humidity?

## EXPERIMENT/DEMONSTRATION #33

### MATERIALS NEEDED:

Sponge
Spring scale
Water
Ring stand

### PROCEDURE:

To understand relative humidity, compare the air to a sponge.

**Step 1:** Weigh a completely dry sponge on a spring scale suspended from a ring stand.

**Step 2:** Remove the sponge and add water until the sponge is soaked but not dripping. Weigh the sponge again and compute the weight of the amount of water that was added. The sponge is saturated; that is, it contains 100% of the moisture it is capable of holding.

**Step 3:** Thoroughly dry the sponge. This time, add one-fourth or one-half of the known amount of water the sponge will hold. It can now be said that the sponge (which represents the air) is 25% or 50% saturated.

If more than the known amount of water is added to the sponge, the excess water will drip from the sponge, and the sponge will now be supersaturated.

# How Can We Determine the Dew Point of the Air?

## EXPERIMENT/DEMONSTRATION #34

### MATERIALS NEEDED:

Cracked ice
Water
Polished can
Thermometer

### PROCEDURE:

Determine the dew point of the air by slowly adding cracked ice to water in a polished can. Measure the temperature with a thermometer.

**At what temperature does moisture first form on the outside of the can?** _____

# How Can We Demonstrate Cloud Forms?

## EXPERIMENT/DEMONSTRATION #35

### PROCEDURE:

Make daily observations of cloud types. If a member of the class has a camera with a good filter, such cloud photographs can be developed into an excellent exhibit.

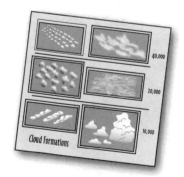

Collect photographs of cloud types and arrange them as a bulletin board exhibit at the same relative levels as they occur in the atmosphere. Point out that observation of cloud movements is a valuable source of information to determine air movements at high altitudes.

# How Can We Make a Cloud?

## EXPERIMENT/DEMONSTRATION #36

### MATERIALS NEEDED:

Two glass milk or juice bottles
Hot water
Cold water
Two ice cubes

### PROCEDURE:

**Step 1:** Fill a milk or juice bottle with hot water.

**Step 2:** Pour out most of the water, leaving about an inch in the bottom.

**Step 3:** Place an ice cube over the mouth of the bottle.

**Step 4:** Repeat the process with cold water.

**What happens in the two glass bottles?** _____

_____

_____

_____

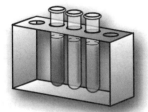

# What Is the Water Cycle?

## EXPERIMENT/DEMONSTRATION #37

### MATERIALS NEEDED:

Water for boiling          Cold water
Drinking glass             Hot plate
Florence flask             Pan

*Adult supervision and the use of safety goggles
are recommended.*

### PROCEDURE:

**Step 1:** Heat some water until it is near the boiling point.

**Step 2:** Pour the hot water into a drinking glass until it is about two-thirds full, and rotate the glass to wet the sides of the glass all the way to the top.

**Step 3:** Now put some cold water into a Florence flask and set the flask on the glass at an angle as shown in the diagram.

Water will evaporate from the surface in the glass and condense on the cold flask. Drops of the condensed water will continue to fall back into the glass. This demonstration makes a simple approach to developing a concept of the water cycle. Evaporation, condensation, and precipitation continue inside the glass just as they do in the outside world.

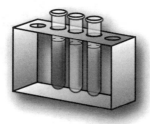

# What Is the Water Cycle? (cont.)

## EXPERIMENT/DEMONSTRATION #38

### MATERIALS NEEDED:

Aquarium
Water
Glass plate

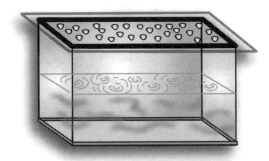

### PROCEDURE:

**Step 1:** Place the aquarium by a sunny window.

**Step 2:** Show how rain is formed by filling the aquarium half-full of water and covering it with a glass plate.

As the sun warms the water, some will evaporate and fill the air above with moisture. Some moisture will gather on the underside of the cool glass plate. When a sufficient amount of water has condensed, it will form into drops and fall back into the bottom of the container like rain.

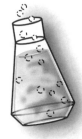

# How Can We Make a Hygrometer?

## EXPERIMENT/DEMONSTRATION #39

### MATERIALS NEEDED:

Two similar thermometers    Board
Length of lamp wick         Small can or bottle
Water                       Electric fan
*Adult supervision is recommended.*

### PROCEDURE:

**Step 1:** Make a hygrometer by mounting two similar thermometers vertically on a board.

**Step 2:** Tie one end of a piece of lamp wick around the bulb of one of the thermometers and immerse the other end of the wick in a small can or bottle of water.

**Step 3:** With a fan, circulate the air about the bulbs of the thermometers to induce faster evaporation and cooling of the wet bulb.

**Step 4:** When no further temperature change is noticed for the wet bulb, record the temperature readings of both the wet and dry bulb thermometers and check the chart below for the relative humidity.

| Dry Bulb Temperature °F | Difference Between Dry and Wet Bulbs °F | | | | | |
|---|---|---|---|---|---|---|
| | 3° | 6° | 9° | 12° | 15° | 18° |
| | Relative Humidity | | | | | |
| 65° | 85% | 70% | 56% | 44% | 31% | 20% |
| 70° | 86% | 72% | 60% | 48% | 36% | 26% |
| 75° | 87% | 74% | 62% | 51% | 40% | 31% |
| 80° | 87% | 75% | 64% | 54% | 44% | 35% |

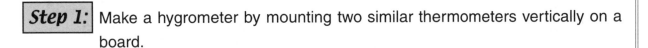

# How Can We Make Smog?

## EXPERIMENT/DEMONSTRATION #40

### MATERIALS NEEDED:

Match
Glass jug
*Adult supervision and the use of safety goggles are recommended.*

### PROCEDURE:

**Step 1:** Hold a lighted match in the mouth of a glass jug. This will "seed" the air within the jug.

**Step 2:** Blow into the jug several times.

**Step 3:** Place the mouth of the jug against the lips, blow hard, and release the pressure suddenly.

**What happens?** _____

_____

_____

_____

**What happens if the jug is blown into again?** _____

_____

_____

# What Is Sleet?

## EXPERIMENT/DEMONSTRATION #41

**MATERIALS NEEDED:**

Small test tube
Thermometer
Crushed ice
Jar
Salt
Water

**PROCEDURE:**

**Step 1:** Sleet is, simply stated, tiny frozen rain drops. To demonstrate this, fill a small test tube with water.

**Step 2:** Place the thermometer in the test tube and record the water temperature.

**Step 3:** Place the test tube with the thermometer in it into a jar of crushed ice and salt.

**What happens to the water in the tube?** _____

_____

_____

# Does Water Exert Pressure?

## EXPERIMENT/DEMONSTRATION #42

### MATERIALS NEEDED:

| | | |
|---|---|---|
| Rubber (from a balloon) | Water | Thistle tube |
| Large beaker | Ruler | Manometer |

### PROCEDURE:

**Step 1:** Fasten a piece of sheet rubber over a thistle tube. (The rubber can be cut from a balloon.)

**Step 2:** Attach the tube to a manometer.

**Step 3:** Hold the end of the thistle tube at various depths under water.

**What happens?** (Use the form at the beginning of this book or your own paper.)

## EXPERIMENT/DEMONSTRATION #43

### MATERIALS NEEDED:

Quart or half-gallon milk carton          Sink with flowing water

### PROCEDURE:

The difference in water pressure on different floors in some buildings is very noticeable. Some students may not know that very tall buildings have water supply tanks above the top floor. A picture showing the rooftops of any older city will reveal many of these tanks. In more modern buildings, these tanks are enclosed by the roof or placed in a tower.

**Step 1:** Punch four holes in a milk carton, one above the other at regular intervals as shown in the diagram. Set the carton in a sink.

**Step 2:** Fill the carton with water and adjust the water supply entering the carton so that the water continues to flow from all four holes in the side of the carton.

**Step 3:** Observe how far water shoots from each hole.

# What Is the Water Table?

## EXPERIMENT/DEMONSTRATION #44

### MATERIALS NEEDED:

Large-bore glass tube    Large, deep beaker
Sand    Water
Narrow strip of wet paper

A simple model that can be set up within a few seconds presents an excellent approach to the concept of the water table.

### PROCEDURE:

**Step 1:** Hold a large-bore glass tube against the side of a large, deep beaker to represent a well.

**Step 2:** Fill the beaker with sand, and pour water on the sand until the water level rises about half as high as the top of the sand. Note that the water level is the same outside the well (glass tube) as it is inside the well.

**Step 3:** Paste a narrow strip of wet paper on the beaker to mark the water level and discuss the term *water table*.

# What Is the Effect of Lowering the Water Table?

## EXPERIMENT/DEMONSTRATION #45

### MATERIALS NEEDED:

Aquarium filled with sand and water with a "well" in one corner and a depression that forms a "pond"
Demonstration pump    Piece of large-bore glass tube
Short piece of rubber tubing    Large beaker
*Adult supervision is recommended.*

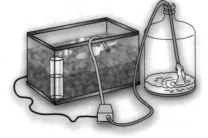

### PROCEDURE:

Use the glass tube as the "well" and make a depression in the sand to form the "pond." Pump water from the glass tube into the beaker. The well and pond go dry as the water is pumped out. When the well and pond have been drained, the water table can be raised again by reversing the position of the pump. A short piece of rubber tubing can be attached to the spout of the pump so that water can be pumped from the beaker back into the well.

# Upon What Does the Height of the Water Table Depend?

## EXPERIMENT/DEMONSTRATION #46

### MATERIALS NEEDED:

Metal can        Rotary can opener
Water            Watch

*Adult supervision and the use of protective gloves are recommended.*

The source of water in the soil is rainfall. The height of the water table, therefore, mainly depends upon how well water penetrates the soil. A large amount of runoff occurs when soils are relatively impervious to water. Most of this runoff water is carried away by streams and does not help raise the water table. To determine the permeability of the soil, perform the following experiment.

### PROCEDURE:

**Step 1:** Cut the top and bottom off a metal can.

**Step 2:** Press the can into the ground to a distance of about one inch and fill it completely with water. Use a watch to determine the time required for all of the water to go into the soil.

**Step 3:** Repeat the above procedure in different places so the data can be summarized into a table and/or graph.

# What Is the Evidence That the Water Table Is Near the Surface?

## ADDITIONAL ACTIVITY

Ask students to mention places where there is evidence that the water table is near the surface. Swampy or marshy locations can usually be found at a distance that is not too far for a short field trip. During a field trip of this kind, one significant observation that can be made is the difference in the vegetation in wet and dry areas. If the field trip is taken in early spring, it will often be possible to find the water table by digging a small hole with a shovel. Attention should be called to the fact that the water table is usually nearer the surface in spring than at other times of the year.

## What Is the Effect of the Water Table on Seedlings?

### EXPERIMENT/DEMONSTRATION #47

#### MATERIALS NEEDED:

Two graduated cylinders    Soil    Water
Two thistle tubes    Beans

#### PROCEDURE:

The effect of the height of the water table on the germination and growth of seedlings can easily be demonstrated as shown on the right. Observe the growth of the seedlings and also observe capillary action in the soil. In addition, it shows that the water table must be constantly replenished because of water lost by evaporation at the surface.

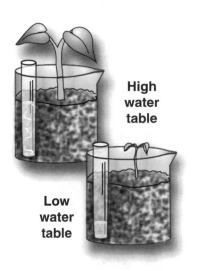

High water table

Low water table

## How Can the Amount of Runoff Water Be Reduced?

### ADDITIONAL ACTIVITY

The importance of reducing the amount of runoff water can be shown by comparing an area protected by vegetation to one that is not so protected. The protected area will be more moist. Water from previous rains will still be helping to maintain the water table in the protected area. The unprotected area will be depleting the water table. Suitable areas for comparison can often be located on or near the school campus or in a nearby park. The effects of unwise farming practices, the building of dams and reservoirs, and the construction of drainage ditches can also be related to the water table. The question of whether or not the local community has a water table problem and what might be done about it should also be considered.

# How Can We Chemically Remove Impurities From Water?

## EXPERIMENT/DEMONSTRATION #48

### MATERIALS NEEDED:

Muddy water       Jar       Alum crystals

### PROCEDURE:

**Step 1:** Put some muddy water in a tall jar.

**Step 2:** Add a small amount of alum crystals.

**Step 3:** Stir the mixture and allow it to settle.

The alum forms a jellylike mass that entangles the dirt particles and carries them down as it settles. This process, which is called **coagulation**, is used by many cities to remove suspended matter from the water supply.

# How Can We Chemically Remove Impurities From Water? (cont.)

## EXPERIMENT/DEMONSTRATION #49

### MATERIALS NEEDED:

Water      Beaker      Burner

*Adult supervision and the use of safety goggles are recommended.*

### PROCEDURE:

**Step 1:** Pour off some of the water obtained from the previous coagulation demonstration.

**Step 2:** Heat a sample in a beaker over a burner to evaporate the water.

**Step 3:** Turn off the burner just as the final water boils away.

**Step 4:** Allow the beaker to cool and examine the contents.

The deposit in the beaker is similar to that which forms inside a teakettle and in boiler pipes. Emphasize that filtering and coagulation do not remove mineral matter.

# How Can We Chemically Remove Impurities From Water? (cont.)

## EXPERIMENT/DEMONSTRATION #50

**MATERIALS NEEDED:**

Large vessel        Sink        Water

Chlorine is added to most city water to destroy bacteria.

**PROCEDURE:**

**Step 1:** Set a large vessel in a sink and quickly half-fill it with cold water. If chlorine is present, it will be possible to smell when sniffing close to the top of the vessel.

**Step 2:** Allow the chlorinated water to stand for half an hour and smell it again. Nearly all of the chlorine will have escaped.

## How Can We Filter Water?

### EXPERIMENT/DEMONSTRATION #51

**MATERIALS NEEDED:**

Large glass funnel        Pebbles            Coarse and fine sand
Ring stand                Muddy water        Beaker

**PROCEDURE:**

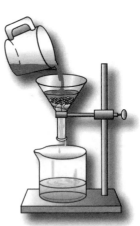

**Step 1:** Support a large glass funnel on a ring stand.

**Step 2:** Fill the funnel with clean pebbles, coarse sand, and fine sand, as shown in the diagram.

**Step 3:** Pour some muddy water through this filter unit.

Call attention to the fact that, although most of the solid impurities have been removed, the water is still not safe for drinking.

# How Can We Distill Water?

## EXPERIMENT/DEMONSTRATION #52

### MATERIALS NEEDED:

Tall, 500 mL beaker        Bent metal platform
50 mL beaker               Evaporating dish
Impure water               Burner or hot plate
*Adult supervision and the use of safety goggles are recommended.*

### PROCEDURE:

**Step 1:** Arrange a simple distillation unit as shown in the diagram.

**Step 2:** Pour some of the impure water into the large beaker and heat until some water collects in the smaller beaker. This water will be practically free from impurities.

**Step 3:** Save the distilled water for subsequent demonstrations.

# What Is the Function of Soap?

## EXPERIMENT/DEMONSTRATION #53

### MATERIALS NEEDED:

Test tube        Cooking oil
Water            Dish soap
*The use of safety goggles is recommended.*

### PROCEDURE:

**Step 1:** Add a few drops of cooking oil to a test tube half filled with water. Shake the tube vigorously. Notice that the oil is broken up into drops that soon come together again.

**Step 2:** Now add a drop of dish soap, shake the tube again, and notice the drops of oil disappear.

   The oil is broken up into very fine droplets, forming an emulsion. These droplets can easily be rinsed away.

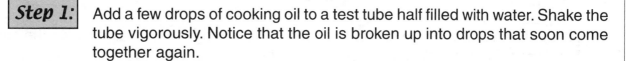

# What Is the Function of Soap? (cont.)

## EXPERIMENT/DEMONSTRATION #54

**MATERIALS NEEDED:**

Cloth          Grease          Water          Soap

**PROCEDURE:**

**Step 1:** Rub some grease on a piece of cloth and try to wash it out with water.

**Step 2:** Repeat with soapy water.

Another effective demonstration is for students to grease their hands and attempt to wash them first in plain tap water and then with soap to remove the grease.

# What Is the Disadvantage of Hard Water?

## EXPERIMENT/DEMONSTRATION #55

**MATERIALS NEEDED:**

Soap flakes          Two beakers
Epsom salt           Water

**PROCEDURE:**

**Step 1:** To make hard water, add a teaspoonful of Epsom salt to a large beaker half full of tap water.

**Step 2:** In a similar beaker half full of water, dissolve some soap flakes.

**Step 3:** Now pour the contents of one beaker into the other, and notice the scum that forms. Feel the scum and notice how sticky it is.

In hard water, much soap is wasted because it combines with chemicals in the water and can no longer perform its cleansing action.

# How Can We Make Water Softer?

## EXPERIMENT/DEMONSTRATION #56

### MATERIALS NEEDED:

| | | |
|---|---|---|
| Washing soda | Borax | Water |
| Liquid dish soap | Four test tubes | Epsom salt |
| Test tube rack | | |

*The use of safety goggles is recommended.*

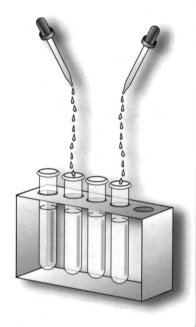

### PROCEDURE:

**Step 1:** Mix a little borax or other water softener in a small quantity of water.

**Step 2:** Make some hard water by adding a few Epsom salt crystals to about a pint of tap water. Now set four test tubes in a rack, each filled about three-quarters full as follows:

1. Hard water plus 10 drops of water softener
2. Hard water with no softener
3. Tap water plus 10 drops of water softener
4. Tap water with no softener

**Step 3:** Add liquid soap to each test tube, drop by drop, shaking well after each drop until lasting suds are formed.

**Step 4:** Summarize the results in a table and interpret.

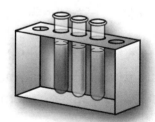

# How Does Changing Air Pressure Affect Objects?

## EXPERIMENT/DEMONSTRATION #57

### MATERIALS NEEDED:

Drinking straw          Ping-pong ball

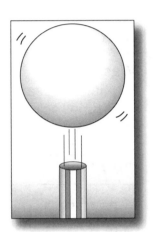

### PROCEDURE:

**Step 1:** Cut a short piece of drinking straw.

**Step 2:** The person with the straw should hold his or her head back so the straw is vertical and then blow hard through the straw.

**Step 3:** Place a ping-pong ball very carefully in the stream of air. It can be held several inches above the straw as long as the air supply lasts.

## EXPERIMENT/DEMONSTRATION #58

### MATERIALS NEEDED:

Support          String
Two apples       Drinking straw

### PROCEDURE:

**Step 1:** Tie strings to two apples and suspend them from a support one or two inches apart.

**Step 2:** Ask students to blow hard through the straw and try to blow the apples farther apart. Instead of moving farther apart, the apples bump together because the air moving between them reduces the air pressure.

# How Does Changing Air Pressure Affect Objects? (cont.)

## EXPERIMENT/DEMONSTRATION #59

### MATERIALS NEEDED:

Balloon        Electric fan        String        Paper clips
*Adult supervision is recommended.*

### PROCEDURE:

**Step 1:** Inflate a toy balloon and close the opening with string.

**Step 2:** Tilt an electric fan upward and place the balloon in the air stream. The pressure of the surrounding air is greater than that in the air stream.

**Step 3:** Attach one or more paper clips to the string and note that the balloon exerts a lifting force.

# How Does Changing Air Pressure Affect Objects? (cont.)

## EXPERIMENT/DEMONSTRATION #60

### MATERIALS NEEDED:

Three sheets of thin cardboard          Drinking straw

### PROCEDURE:

**Step 1:** Bend down the edges of a piece of cardboard so it is held about one-half inch above a table.

**Step 2:** With a drinking straw, blow air under the piece of cardboard. Explain what happens in terms of the relative pressures of still air and moving air.

**Step 3:** Roll a piece of cardboard until it is permanently curved, and set it upright on a table.

**Step 4:** With another card, brush air past the convex surface and note the direction in which the card falls.

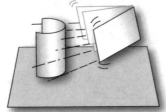

# How Is a Plane Lifted?

## EXPERIMENT/DEMONSTRATION #61

### MATERIALS NEEDED:

Model airplane
Support (for plane)
Modeling clay
Platform balance
Electric fan
*Adult supervision is recommended.*

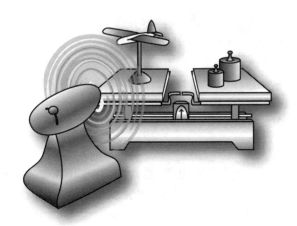

### PROCEDURE:

**Step 1:** Fasten a small model plane above one platform of a platform balance as shown in the diagram.

**Step 2:** Use modeling clay or some other convenient means of holding it in position. Then balance the scale.

**Step 3:** Direct air from an electric fan toward the wing.

**What happens?** _____

_____

_____

_____

_____

_____

_____

# How Is Thrust Provided by Propellers?

## EXPERIMENT/DEMONSTRATION #62

### MATERIALS NEEDED:

Smooth board
Electric fan
Three round pencils
*Adult supervision is recommended.*

The force that drives airplanes forward is known as **thrust**. In conventional airplanes, thrust is provided by the propeller. The effect of this force can be easily observed.

### PROCEDURE:

**Step 1:** On a smooth table, place a smooth board on top of three round pencils, making sure the board will roll easily.

**Step 2:** Place a portable electric fan on top of the board, and turn on the fan.

**What happens?** _____

_____

_____

_____

_____

_____

_____

# How Is Lift Provided by an Airplane?

## EXPERIMENT/DEMONSTRATION #63

**MATERIALS NEEDED:**

Scissors       Paper

**PROCEDURE:**

**Step 1:** Cut a strip of paper nine inches long and two inches wide.

**Step 2:** Hold it by the narrow end and blow across the upper surface of the paper.

**What happens to the paper?** _____

_____

_____

_____

# How Can We Demonstrate Drag?

## EXPERIMENT/DEMONSTRATION #64

### MATERIALS NEEDED:

Cardboard          Tape or modeling clay          Candle
*Adult supervision is recommended.*

### PROCEDURE:

**Step 1:** To show drag, obtain a piece of cardboard about three inches square.

**Step 2:** Light a candle and place it vertically on a table or dish.

**Step 3:** Place the cardboard about two or three inches from the candle and secure it with a bit of clay or tape.

**Step 4:** Blow hard against the secured card.

### What happens to the flame? _____

_____

_____

# How Can We Demonstrate Drag? (cont.)

## EXPERIMENT/DEMONSTRATION #65

### MATERIALS NEEDED:

Flexible cardboard        Glue and/or paper clips        Candle
*Adult supervision is recommended.*

### PROCEDURE:

**Step 1:** Obtain a piece of flexible cardboard about 3 inches by ten inches.

**Step 2:** Bend the ends of the cardboard as shown and fasten them with glue and/or paper clips.

**Step 3:** Place the cardboard near the candle with the clipped or glued ends nearest the candle.

**Step 4:** Blow against the curved end.

**What happens?** (Use the form at the beginning of this book or your own paper.)

# How Can We Demonstrate Thrust in Jets and Rockets?

## EXPERIMENT/DEMONSTRATION #66

### MATERIALS NEEDED:

Balloon

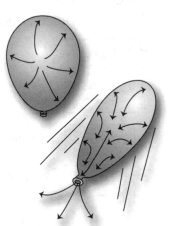

Rockets and jet-propelled aircraft, as well as propeller-driven planes, move forward by means of **thrust**. The thrust of rockets and jets is caused by the flow of hot gases from the exhaust.

### PROCEDURE:

Blow up a balloon and release it. The rapid escape of air pushes the balloon in the opposite direction. This illustrates the fundamental principle of jet propulsion.

## How Can We Demonstrate Thrust in Jets and Rockets? (cont.)

### EXPERIMENT/DEMONSTRATION #67

**MATERIALS NEEDED:**

Smooth wire            1 1/2-inch square of paper
Two paper clips        Tape
Long balloon           String

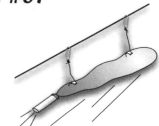

**PROCEDURE:**

**The paper tube may be pinched to control speed.**

**Step 1:** Construct a toy jet balloon as shown in the illustration. Stretch a smooth wire or string across a room.

**Step 2:** Attach lengths of string to a long balloon so it hangs parallel to the wire.

**Step 3:** Place paper clips on the wire and blow up the balloon. As it deflates, the balloon will be propelled along the wire.

The speed of the balloon rocket may be modified by squeezing the opening of the tube. (The tube is made of a 1 1/2-inch square of paper, shaped around a pencil, taped, and inserted into the neck of the balloon.)

### EXPERIMENT/DEMONSTRATION #68

**MATERIALS NEEDED:**

Small bottle (with cork)      Stand          Thread
Rubbing alcohol              Candle
*Adult supervision and the use of safety goggles are recommended.*

**PROCEDURE:**

**Step 1:** Suspend a small bottle by two threads.

**Step 2:** Place a tablespoonful of rubbing alcohol in the bottle and cork it.

**Step 3:** Carefully heat the bottle with a candle flame.

### What happens to the bottle as the cork pops out?

(Use the form at the beginning of this book or your own paper.)

# How Can We Demonstrate Thrust in Jets and Rockets? (cont.)

## EXPERIMENT/DEMONSTRATION #69

### MATERIALS NEEDED:

Small empty can (with lid)
Wire
Candle
Hammer
Nail
Pan of water
Small plastic container that will float
*Adult supervision and the use of safety goggles are recommended.*

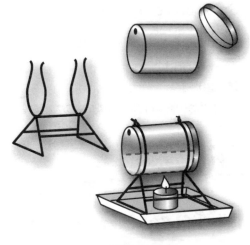

### PROCEDURE:

**Step 1:** Build a simple jet engine. With a hammer and nail, punch a small hole near the edge of the bottom of a small can.

**Step 2:** Mount the can so it will stand horizontally on wires with the hole at the top.

**Step 3:** Half-fill the can with water and replace the cover.

**Step 4:** Mount the can on top of the plastic dish or container so the candle flame will be directly under it. When the water boils, steam will issue forth from the pinhole jet. To do this, the steam must also push forward on the "boiler." Because of this push, the boat will speed across the pan of water.

# How Can We Demonstrate Thrust in Jets and Rockets? (cont.)

## EXPERIMENT/DEMONSTRATION #70

**MATERIALS NEEDED:**

Small bottle (with cork)
Baking soda
Vinegar
Two round pencils
Paper
*Adult supervision is recommended.*

**PROCEDURE:**

**Step 1:** Lay a small bottle on two round pencils so the bottle rolls easily.

**Step 2:** Wrap a teaspoonful of baking soda in a small piece of paper and place it in the bottle.

**Step 3:** Place a tablespoonful of vinegar in the bottle and cork it loosely.

**What happens?** _____

_____

_____

_____

_____

_____

_____

_____

# How Can We Demonstrate Thrust in Jets and Rockets? (cont.)

## EXPERIMENT/DEMONSTRATION #71

### MATERIALS NEEDED:

Rubber tubing
Funnel (metal or glass)
Glass tubing
Water
*Use of safety goggles and protective gloves
are recommended.*

Show that a jet of water, as well as a jet of air, can cause
a thrust.

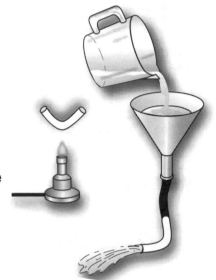

### PROCEDURE:

**Step 1:** Attach a piece of rubber tubing about one foot long to the end of a glass or
metal funnel.

**Step 2:** Heat a piece of glass tubing about four inches long and bend it to form a
right angle.

**Step 3:** Attach the bent glass tube to the lower end of the rubber tube.

**Step 4:** Hold the funnel upright and pour water into it.

**What happens?** _____

_____

_____

_____

_____

# How Can We Demonstrate Thrust in Jets and Rockets? (cont.)

## EXPERIMENT/DEMONSTRATION #72

### MATERIALS NEEDED:

Large coffee can
Water
String
Hammer
Nail
*Adult supervision is recommended.*

### PROCEDURE:

**Step 1:** Punch several nail holes around a metal coffee can near the bottom.

**Step 2:** Push the nail sideways in the same direction before removing it from each hole.

**Step 3:** Suspend the can as shown in the diagram and fill the can with water.

**What happens?** _____

_____

_____

_____

_____

_____

_____

_____

# How Can We Demonstrate the Principle of the Helicopter?

## EXPERIMENT/DEMONSTRATION #73

### MATERIALS NEEDED:

Paper          Scissors          Paper clip

### PROCEDURE:

**Step 1:** Cut out a piece of paper as shown in the diagram.

**Step 2:** Fold over the bottom section as shown and fasten it with a paper clip.

**Step 3:** Throw the device into the air, and it will spin rapidly as it falls.

    The spin causes an upward thrust, but this is enough thrust to reduce the rate of fall. Helicopters can use this method of landing in the event of engine failure.

## EXPERIMENT/DEMONSTRATION #74

### MATERIALS NEEDED:

Paper          Scissors          Straight pin          Pencil

### PROCEDURE:

**Step 1:** Make four cuts in a sheet of paper five inches square as shown.

**Step 2:** Bend the four corners toward the center and put a straight pin through the five holes indicated to form a pinwheel.

**Step 3:** The point of the pin is then placed in the end of the eraser of an ordinary pencil.

**Step 4:** When this device is dropped from a window or stairwell, its fall is slowed down by the upward thrust of the revolving pinwheel.

    Many times, helicopters can land safely even when the motor stops.

# How Can We Demonstrate the Principle of the Helicopter? (cont.)

## EXPERIMENT/DEMONSTRATION #75

### MATERIALS NEEDED:

Soft wood          Dowel rod
Drill and bit to drill a hole the same diameter as the dowel rod
*Adve supervision and the use of safety goggles are recommended.*

### PROCEDURE:

**Step 1:**  From a strip of soft wood six inches long, one inch wide, and one-fourth inch thick, cut away the edges as shown in the diagram.

**Step 2:**  Bore a small hole in the center and fit a dowel rod into it.

**Step 3:**  Spin the dowel between your hands very rapidly, and the device will rise into the air as a helicopter does. The rotating propeller blades push the air downward, and the reaction, or thrust, forces the helicopter upward.

Some helicopters have a motor-driven propeller. In some, jet engines are mounted at the ends of the wings. These operate on a principle similar to that of a rotary lawn sprinkler.

Try spinning the helicopter model at a slight angle, and it will travel in a sideways direction. The movements of a real helicopter are controlled by varying the tilt and pitch of the rotating wings.

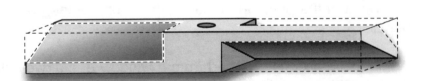

## How Can We Demonstrate the Function of Elevators and Rudders?

### EXPERIMENT/DEMONSTRATION #76

**MATERIALS NEEDED:**

Drinking straw          Paste          Index card
Bottle (with cork)      Scissors       Cardboard
Thumbtack

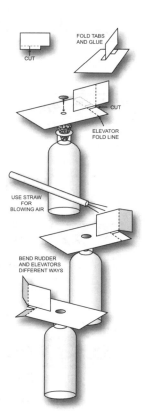

**PROCEDURE:**

**Step 1:** On a three-by-five-inch index card, paste a vertical cardboard fin as shown in the diagram.

**Step 2:** Leave the rear portion of the fin free by extending it beyond the card. Find the point at which the card balances, and push a thumbtack through it into the cork of a bottle. The card should now turn easily.

**Step 3:** Blow through a drinking straw, directing the air across the top of the card. Turn the card slightly and blow across it. It turns back and faces the wind, illustrating the function of the vertical fin of an airplane.

**Step 4:** Bend the unattached portion of the fin to the left along the vertical dotted line shown in the diagram. Again blow air over the cardboard. Bend it to the right and repeat. Note the movement of the card. This illustrates the function of the rudder.

If the rudder is turned to the right, the wind forces the tail to the left, while the nose moves to the right. The opposite effect is noted if the rudder is turned to the left.

**Step 5:** Make the two cuts on the rear of the card. Bend the two portions of the trailing edge of the card upward to represent the elevators in raised position.

**Step 6:** Blow across the top of the card and note that the rear of the card goes down. Bend the elevators down and repeat.

**Step 7:** Adjust both the elevators and the rudders in different ways to show how they work together.

# How Can We Demonstrate the Function of the Ailerons?

## EXPERIMENT/DEMONSTRATION #77

### MATERIALS NEEDED:

Cardboard          Scissors          Thread

### PROCEDURE:

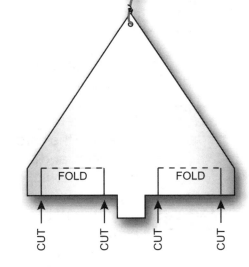

**Step 1:** Remove the cardboard from the back of an ordinary writing tablet.

**Step 2:** Cut a plane model similar to the diagram so the wingspread and length from nose to tail are both about eight inches.

**Step 3:** Attach a string about one foot long to the nose of the plane. Allow the plane to hang straight down on the end of the string.

**Step 4:** Pull the string upward slowly. Note that the plane has little or no spin.

**Step 5:** Make the cuts on the rear of the wings as shown. Bend one edge down and one up.

**Step 6:** Now pull the string upward slowly and note the direction of spin. Reverse the position of the bent parts and again note the direction of spin. This shows the function of the ailerons.

# Air Safety: For What Are Seat Belts Used?

## EXPERIMENT/DEMONSTRATION #78

### MATERIALS NEEDED:

Doll (or other small object)          Brick
Roller skate or small wagon          String

### PROCEDURE:

**Step 1:** Place a doll or other small object on a roller skate or in a small wagon and put a brick or similar heavy object in its path.

**Step 2:** Push the skate/wagon so it rolls along the desktop or floor and hits the brick. Note what happens to the doll when the skate/wagon is stopped.

**Step 3:** Tie the doll to the skate/wagon and repeat the experiment. Note that there is now little or no forward movement of the doll when the skate/wagon stops.

## How Can We Make a Parachute?

### EXPERIMENT/DEMONSTRATION #79

### MATERIALS NEEDED:

Handkerchief          String          Spool

### PROCEDURE:

**Step 1:** Tie a string about eight inches long to each corner of a large handkerchief.

**Step 2:** Fasten a lightweight object, such as a thread spool, to the strings.

**Step 3:** Wrap the handkerchief and strings around the spool and throw it up into the air. As it falls, the parachute will open and slow the fall of the spool. It may be necessary to increase or decrease the weight to make the parachute open properly.

# What Is the Principle of Artificial Satellites?
# What Is Meant by Centrifugal Force?

## EXPERIMENT/DEMONSTRATION #80

### MATERIALS NEEDED:

Stout cord          Two, one-hole rubber stoppers

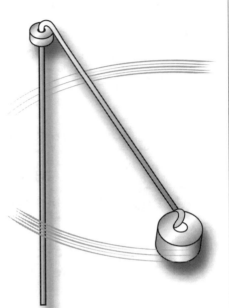

Students ask many questions about why artificial satellites continue to revolve about the earth. The demonstration in the diagram should provide the basis for an understanding of this problem.

### PROCEDURE:

**Step 1:** Tie a stout cord, several feet in length, to a one-hole rubber stopper.

**Step 2:** Run the other end of the cord through another rubber stopper.

**Step 3:** Holding the second rubber stopper in one hand, swing the stopper at the end of the string in a wide circle to represent the revolution of the moon about the earth.

**What does the pull on the cord represent? The outward pull?**

_____

_____

**How does the moon continue to revolve about the earth?**

_____

_____

**What happens when the stopper is swung in a wide circle and the cord is pulled quickly to shorten its orbit?** _____

_____

# How Should We Approach the Study of Time?

## EXPERIMENT/DEMONSTRATION #81

The study of time can be approached in an interesting way by showing how the ability to estimate time varies. Divide the class into two groups, and ask one group to sit quietly with their eyes closed and to raise their hands at the end of two minutes. Members of the other group can observe the variation in the estimates. Repeat the procedure with the groups interchanged.

Discuss ways of estimating time, using pulse rate or respiration rate, and repeat the procedure after the students have recognized the need for using some rhythmic procedure, such as counting seconds by saying, "one thousand and one, one thousand and two," etc.

# What Are Some Devices for Keeping Time?

## EXPERIMENT/DEMONSTRATION #82

### MATERIALS NEEDED:

Weight(s)          String          Ring stand

Demonstrate some of the devices for measuring time. An egg timer uses the same principle as does an hourglass. Similar water clocks can easily be made. Some students may be interested in making various types of sundials.

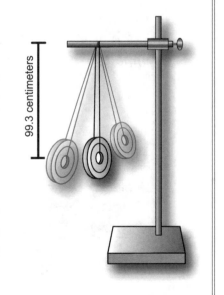

### PROCEDURE:

Use a string and weight to make a pendulum that beats seconds. A pendulum that is 99.3 centimeters in length from the point of suspension to the center of the weight will require one second to swing in each direction. It will, therefore, have a period of two seconds.

# Upon What Does the Period of a Pendulum Depend?

## EXPERIMENT/DEMONSTRATION #83

### MATERIALS NEEDED:

Weight            String                    Fine steel wire
Ring stand        Watch or alarm clock

### PROCEDURE:

**Step 1:** Use the procedure shown in the diagram to demonstrate that the period depends on the length of the pendulum but not on the weight. Raise the pendulum while it is swinging by pulling on the string.

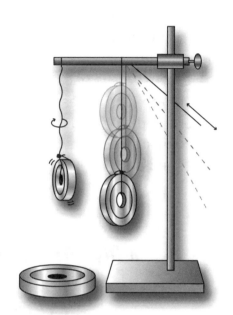

**Step 2:** Try different sizes of weights. Suspend a weight by means of a fine steel wire as shown to the right.

**Step 3:** Rotate the weight and release it.

Torsion clocks operate on this principle. Examine the hairspring and escapement in a watch or alarm clock. Point out that a little of the energy stored up in the mainspring is imparted to the escapement every time the clock ticks.

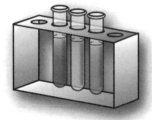

# What Are the Time Zones in the United States?

## EXPERIMENT/DEMONSTRATION #84

### MATERIALS NEEDED:

Map of the United States showing the standard time zones

### PROCEDURE:

**Step 1:** On a map of the United States showing the standard time zones, locate the meridians that determine the standard time used in each zone.

**Step 2:** Discuss the reasons why time zones are necessary and why the borders are so irregular.

**Step 3:** Ask students to give examples of radio and television programs that illustrate the time differences across the country.

**Step 4:** Make a diagram explaining how the zones shift when daylight saving time is used.

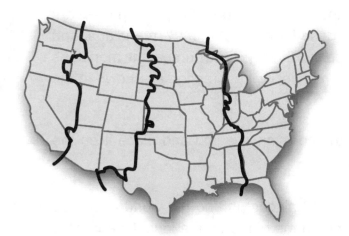

# How Can We Make a Time Cone?

## EXPERIMENT/DEMONSTRATION #85

### MATERIALS NEEDED:

Heavy paper          Scissors          Fine-point marker
Globe                Paper clip

Make a time cone that will sit on a globe with the base on the parallel of latitude of your community.

### PROCEDURE:

**Step 1:** Draw a circle on a piece of heavy paper, and then cut the disk along a radius.

**Step 2:** Overlap one edge to form a cone as shown in the diagram.

**Step 3:** Adjust the circumference of the base of the cone so it rests on the earth approximately on the 42° parallel.

**Step 4:** Close the cone with a paper clip and put a mark on the base for each of the 15° meridians, and then open up the cone and number the meridians in a counterclockwise direction as shown in the diagram.

**Step 5:** Form the cone once again and place it on the globe.

**Step 6:** Select 8–10 places around the world and observe the time for each. Set the cone on the globe so the local time is on the 75° meridian. Point out that most of the world's time zones are centered on the meridians that are divisible by 15, such as 75, 105, and 135.

# How Can We Use a Sextant to Measure Latitude?

## EXPERIMENT/DEMONSTRATION #86

### MATERIALS NEEDED:

Thumbtack          Cardboard protractor          Straight stick
Thread             Nail                          Flashlight

### PROCEDURE:

**Step 1:** Make the simple sextant shown in the diagram and sight along the top of the stick to the North Star.

**Step 2:** When the North Star is in line with the stick, press the thumb and finger over the thread and protractor to hold it in position. The latitude can then be read directly from the scale with a flashlight for illumination.

**Step 3:** Demonstrate the sextant in the classroom by showing where the plumb line would fall if the observation was made at the equator and at the North Pole. Sextants like those used for navigation can be inexpensive. This type can be used to determine latitude by "shooting the sun."

## How Can We Make a Sextant?

### EXPERIMENT/DEMONSTRATION #87

### MATERIALS NEEDED:

Drinking straw        Cardboard protractor          Pin
Pencil or dowel       Bent pin for pointer
Needle for pointer    Two protractors mounted on a wood base

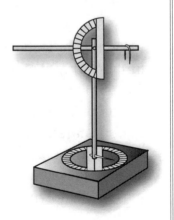

### PROCEDURE:

A simple device that can be used both as a sextant and as a transit is shown in the diagram. One or more students may wish to construct one as a project.

# How Can We Collect and Study Rocks?

## EXPERIMENT/DEMONSTRATION #88

### MATERIALS NEEDED:

Ask each student to bring in one rock. A satisfactory sampling of local rocks can usually be obtained.

### PROCEDURE:

**Step 1:** Place similar specimens of rocks together, dividing the rocks into groups according to differences in shape, color, and other characteristics. Try to discover several different ways in which the rocks that have been collected can be grouped.

**Step 2:** Select a single rock and try to learn as much about it as possible by careful observation alone. If a rock is flat, it is probably a piece of a layer of sediment that was laid down in water long ago and has since hardened. If it appears to be made up of sand grains cemented together, it is probably sandstone. If the rock is rounded, the wearing off of sharp corners is very likely the result of stream action. Granite-like rocks that have crystals of different colors were pushed up from deep in the earth long ago and cooled slowly. Rocks that differ greatly from most of the rocks found in the community were probably carried in by a glacier.

Careful observation of rock specimens using the developmental technique will serve to interest students in the further study of rocks. Many beginners will be curious to know the names of different rocks, but the identification of rocks will be of far less value than the development of their stories through careful observation of their characteristics. Identification, except for the most common kinds, might be avoided with beginners, since even experts cannot be sure of the name of a rock without testing it in a laboratory.

# How Can Rock Collections Be Made?

## EXPERIMENT/DEMONSTRATION #89

### MATERIALS NEEDED:

| | | |
|---|---|---|
| Box | String | Nail |
| Hammer | Rocks | Adhesive tape |

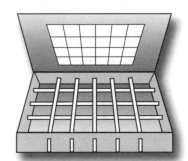

### PROCEDURE:

Encourage students to start small rock collections of their own. A good rock collection box can be purchased at a discount store or made from a cardboard box with a lid. For beginners, it is best to keep the collections small and to confine them largely to local rocks. Students who have a special interest might want to learn how to use more elaborate techniques.

### To make a rock collection box:

**Step 1:** Use a hammer and nail to punch evenly spaced holes in the box a short distance from the bottom.

**Step 2:** Run strings through the holes and around the bottom of the box and tie them tightly on the outside. The strings will then hold the specimens in position.

**Step 3:** Cut small squares of adhesive tape and paste one square on each of the specimens collected and number each specimen.

**Step 4:** Next, make a key with a space for the name of each rock. Write in the names of any rocks that are known and paste the key on the cover of the box. Blank spaces can be filled in later if and when the names of the rocks are learned.

** Egg cartons are also convenient for small rock collections. Keys showing the position of each rock can be pasted on the inside or outside cover.

# What Is the Test for Limestone?

## EXPERIMENT/DEMONSTRATION #90

### MATERIALS NEEDED:

Lemon juice        Tray or pan        Eyedropper

### PROCEDURE:

Some specimens collected will very likely resemble limestone. While scientists who study rocks (geologists) use another acid called hydrochloric acid for this test, lemon juice works almost as well and is much safer.

**Step 1:** Place several specimens in a tray or pan.

**Step 2:** The test for limestone is to drop lemon juice on the surface of several specimens. Those that effervesce, or bubble, are limestone, and the gas given off is carbon dioxide.

# What Do Crystals Look Like?

## EXPERIMENT/DEMONSTRATION #91

### MATERIALS NEEDED:

Small quantity of sand and broken rock
Low-power microscope or good hand lens

### PROCEDURE:

Examine a small quantity of sand and freshly broken rocks under a low-power microscope or a good hand lens. The almost colorless crystals of sand are those of the mineral quartz, the most common mineral on Earth. Crystals of other minerals can also usually be found in sand. Crystals of different minerals will differ in size, shape, and color.

# What Are the Effects of Water on Rocks?

## EXPERIMENT/DEMONSTRATION #92

### MATERIALS NEEDED:

Small, freshly broken pieces of rock
Jar with a lid, half-filled with clear water

### PROCEDURE:

**Step 1:** Place some small, freshly broken pieces of rock in a jar half-filled with clear water.

**Step 2:** Close the lid of the jar and shake it 100 times.

**What happens to the water in the jar?**

_____

_____

_____

_____

_____

**What happens after the jar has been shaken 1,000 times?**

_____

_____

_____

_____

_____

# What Are the Effects of Water on Rocks? (cont.)

## EXPERIMENT/DEMONSTRATION #93

### MATERIALS NEEDED:

A brick or part of a curb that shows evidence of weathering
Pebbles from a stream that runs over a gravel or rock bed

### PROCEDURE:

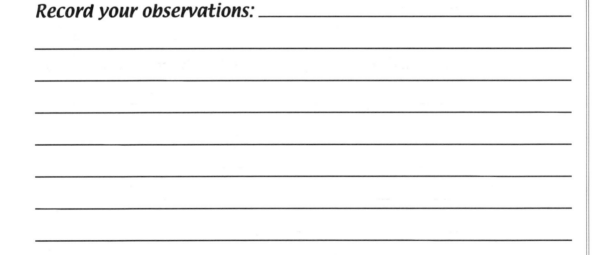

**Step 1:** Find a brick or part of a curb that shows evidence of weathering.

**Step 2:** Collect pebbles from a stream that runs over a gravel or rock bed.

**Step 3:** Note their shapes and textures.

**Step 4:** Rub pieces of different rocks together and note that all rocks are not of the same hardness.

### Record your observations: _____

_____

_____

_____

_____

_____

_____

_____

# How Are New Rocks Formed?

## EXPERIMENT/DEMONSTRATION #94

### PROCEDURE:

What happens to rock particles when rocks are broken and worn away? Observe the work done by running water on or near the school grounds when it rains. Call attention to the mud and small rocks that are carried away by streams, especially when the soil is not protected by a cover of vegetation.

The importance of soil conservation should be developed at this point. Find examples of destructive erosion near the school and discuss means of preventing erosion.

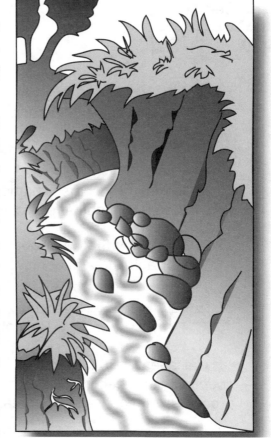

Since mud remains in running water as long as it keeps moving, a great deal of rock material finds its way into lakes or oceans. When the muddy water loses its forward motion, the rock particles settle to the bottom. The larger particles settle first, followed by the smaller. During times of flooding, which usually occur about once a year, enough material settles in the still water to make a layer. Each year a new layer of this sediment is deposited. As time goes on, the particles become pressed and cemented together and finally change into layers of rock.

About four-fifths of the land surface of the earth is covered with layers of rock that were laid down in water. These rocks are called sedimentary rocks. Changes in the levels of the oceans and continents have pushed many of these rocks upward where we see them today.

# How Are New Rocks Formed? (cont.)

## EXPERIMENT/DEMONSTRATION #95

### MATERIALS NEEDED:

Large, wide-mouth jar          Coarse sand or gravel
Fine sand                      Soil
Water                          Spoon or stick for stirring
Tube for siphoning

Sediments settle in water to form layers.

### PROCEDURE:

**Step 1:** Stir a small amount of coarse sand or gravel with some finer sand and soil and add water.

**Step 2:** Pour mixture into a wide-mouth jar.

Notice that the coarser particles settle to the bottom first, followed by the finer particles.

**Step 3:** When the water above the sediment becomes clear, siphon most of it off and add another layer in the same way.

**Step 4:** Additional layers may be added until the jar is nearly full. The layer structure may then be clearly observed through the glass.

Call attention to the fact that lakes and ponds are rapidly disappearing all over the country as they become filled with sediment. Removal of vegetative cover hastens this process. How can we save our lakes and ponds?

## Additional Activity

On an outline map of the United States, locate the mouths of the larger rivers. Indicate the regions offshore where sedimentary rocks are probably forming today.

# How Are Fossils Formed?

## EXPERIMENT/DEMONSTRATION #96

### MATERIALS NEEDED:

Plaster of Paris            Cup, jar, or can
Water                      Greased mold or paper baking cups
*Optional:* Paints and decorations

### PROCEDURE:

**Step 1:** Demonstrate the making of a plaster of Paris cast. First, make a rough estimate of the amount of plaster of Paris mixture desired and pour one-third of this amount of water in a cup, jar, or can.

**Step 2:** Sprinkle plaster of Paris into the water <u>without stirring</u> until small "islands" appear above the surface. This method will give the right proportion of plaster of Paris and water.

Notice that the coarser particles settle to the bottom first, followed by the finer particles.

**Step 3:** Stir the mixture gently with a stick or spoon until smooth. It should have the consistency of melted ice cream or pancake batter.

**Step 4:** Pour the mixture into a greased mold or paper inserts used for muffins. The mixture will soon harden because the plaster of Paris unites chemically with the water.

**Step 5:** If paper baking cups have been used, they can easily be removed from the casts because they are coated with paraffin wax. Such casts may be painted and decorated as desired and make attractive paperweights.

Use the following table as a basis for a discussion of how some common sedimentary rocks are formed.

| Sediment | Process | Sedimentary |
|---|---|---|
| Gravel | Cemented | Conglomerate |
| Shells | Cemented | Limestone |
| Sand | Cemented and pressed | Sandstone |
| Clay or mud | Cemented and pressed | Shale |
| Twigs and leaves | Pressed | Coal |

# How Are Fossils Formed? (cont.)

## EXPERIMENT/DEMONSTRATION #97

### MATERIALS NEEDED:

Glass or smooth board   Plaster of Paris*
Leaf   Petroleum jelly
Water   Modeling clay
Paper, plastic, or thin cardboard

### PROCEDURE:

**Step 1:** Cover a leaf with petroleum jelly and lay it on a pane of glass or a smooth board.

**Step 2:** Around the leaf, place a circular strip of paper, plastic, or thin cardboard and press modeling clay against this collar to hold it in position.

**Step 3:** Pour about one-half inch of plaster of Paris batter over the leaf.

**Step 4:** In about 15 minutes, the paper and leaf can be removed, and an excellent leaf print will result. This illustrates the process of the formation of one type of fossil.

*See page 79 for directions for plaster of Paris.

## Additional Activities

**1.** Cover a shell such as a clam shell with petroleum jelly and pour wet plaster of Paris on it as was done in making a leaf print.

**2.** Look for leaf prints in soft coal. Imprints of fern leaves are commonly found.

**3.** Look through the classroom rock collection for evidence of fossils. Try to find additional fossil-bearing specimens to add to the plaster of Paris collection.

# What Effects Do Plants Have on Rocks?

## EXPERIMENT/DEMONSTRATION #98

### MATERIALS NEEDED:

Straight-sided baking pan or a wooden frame resting on a pane of glass
Plaster of Paris*                   Petroleum jelly
Water                               Sprouted peas or beans
Wet paper towels                    Terrarium

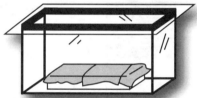

### PROCEDURE:

**Step 1:** Make a one-inch-thick slab of plaster of Paris either in a straight-sided baking pan coated with petroleum jelly or by pouring the plaster into a wooden frame resting on a pane of glass.

**Step 2:** After the plaster has hardened, remove it from the mold.

**Step 3:** Lay sprouted peas or bean seeds on the smooth side of the plaster and cover them with wet paper towels. Keep the slab (and seeds) in a terrarium so that the toweling stays moist.

**Step 4:** After several days, remove the seeds.

*See page 79 for directions for plaster of Paris.

### What happened to the surface of the plaster? Why?

(Use the form at the beginning of this book or your own paper.)

## Additional Activity

Find rocks or rock ledges where mosses and lichens are growing. Scrape some of the plants off and notice that bits of rock flake off, loosened by the chemical action of the plants. A short field trip to see such a rock is an interesting learning activity.

# How Does Water Wear Away the Earth's Surface in Some Places and Build It Up in Others?

## EXPERIMENT/DEMONSTRATION #99

### MATERIALS NEEDED:

Several cans or flower pots          Loose soil
Coins or flat stones                 Large pan
Water ("Rain")

### PROCEDURE:

**Step 1:** Make small drainage holes in the bottoms of several cans or flower pots and fill them with loose soil.

**Step 2:** Press down the soil so that it is even with the edges of the can or flower pot.

**Step 3:** Place coins or flat stones on the surface of the soil as shown in the diagram.

**Step 4:** Set each can in a large pan and sprinkle it with water. Continue the simulated rain until a change can be noted in the surface of the soil.

**Step 5:** Repeat this procedure, but set the cans of soil outdoors during a rain.

**What happens to the soil?**

(Use the form at the beginning of this book or your own paper.)

## EXPERIMENT/DEMONSTRATION #100

### MATERIALS NEEDED:

Sand and clay          Large tray          Watering can

### PROCEDURE:

**Step 1:** Build up a pile of sand and clay in a tray or other large vessel.

**Step 2:** Sprinkle it gently with a watering can. Note the erosion, the transportation of rock particles, and deposits made by the little streams that form.

# How Does Water Wear Away the Earth's Surface in Some Places and Build It Up in Others? (cont.)

## EXPERIMENT/DEMONSTRATION #101

### MATERIALS NEEDED:

Flower pot
Dripping faucet

Sandy soil or loam
Basin

### PROCEDURE:

**Step 1:** Fill a flower pot with sandy soil or loam.

**Step 2:** Set the pot of soil in a basin under a dripping faucet for an hour or more. Notice how the clay and inorganic matter is removed from the surface by the falling drops.

## EXPERIMENT/DEMONSTRATION #102

### MATERIALS NEEDED:

Jar lid or saucer
Large sheet of paper

Pencil
Eyedropper

Soil

### PROCEDURE:

**Step 1:** To demonstrate the impact of a raindrop, set a jar lid or saucer of soil in the center of a large sheet of paper.

**Step 2:** With an eyedropper, release a few drops of water from a height of several feet on the soil and note the amount of soil that is splashed out on the paper.

**Step 3:** Place an obstacle such as a pencil in the path of the falling drops. This is comparable to a plant breaking the force of the water.

# How Does Water Wear Away the Earth's Surface in Some Places and Build It Up in Others? (cont.)

## EXPERIMENT/DEMONSTRATION #103

### MATERIALS NEEDED:

Several metal pans (such as baking tins)
Paper towels
Fine, dry soil          Flat sticks or "laths"
White paint or white paper

### PROCEDURE:

#### PART 1

**Step 1:** Punch holes in the bottoms of several metal pans, such as old baking tins.

**Step 2:** Cover the inside of the tins with paper towels and fill each with fine, dry soil.

**Step 3:** Just before a rain, set them out in different places on the school grounds where they will have different degrees of protection from the rain. After the rain, observe the soil in each tin.

#### PART 2

**Step 1:** Rain or splash sticks also show raindrop erosion. Paint some flat sticks or "laths" with white paint or tack pieces of white paper to them. Point one end of each stick so that it can be driven into the soil more easily.

**Step 2:** Before a rain, put out the rain sticks in various places around the school grounds, such as on bare ground, in grass, under a tree, near the building, or under the eaves.

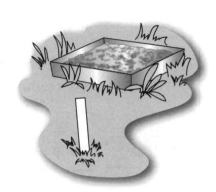

**Step 3:** After a rain, go out and observe the soil splashes on the sticks. Measure their distances from the ground. Tabulate this information and try to account for the differences in the heights of the splashes.

# How Does Water Wear Away the Earth's Surface in Some Places and Build It Up in Others? (cont.)

## Additional Activities

**1.** After a heavy rain, collect jars of muddy water from a stream or from the gutter along the street. Let the water settle to see how much sediment it carried.

**2.** Explore the school grounds for evidence of the transportation of soil by water. Sediment is often deposited along walks and driveways and in low places on the lawn.

**3.** To show which materials in soil are carried away more readily, put some soil in a large jar half-filled with water. Shake the jar vigorously and then let the contents settle. What happens?

**4.** Visit a stream and look for evidence of transportation of the soil by water, such as the muddiness of the stream, worn-away rocks, soil deposited in new places, and pieces of the bank broken off. Notice that the flat rocks in the bottoms of streams are tilted in the opposite direction of the stream's flow.

**5.** Observe how strong the force of a single raindrop can be by dropping colored water onto white paper from varying heights. Using an eyedropper, drop water that has been colored with food coloring onto a sheet of white paper one droplet at a time. Drop three droplets of water from each of three different heights. Measure the spatter pattern of each droplet. Graph the spatter size and drop height, and determine if there are any patterns in the data you have collected. In general, what happens as the drop height increases?

# How Can We Demonstrate the Formation of Stalactites and Stalagmites in Caves?

## EXPERIMENT/DEMONSTRATION #104

### MATERIALS NEEDED:

Cord          Water          Two small vessels
Epsom salt

### PROCEDURE:

**Step 1:** Study pictures of caves and possibly visit caves with guided tours in the vicinity. Account for the formation of caves and sinkholes.

**Step 2:** Closely related to cave formation is the formation of stalactites and stalagmites. The formation of miniature stalactites and stalagmites can be demonstrated by laying a cord between two small vessels filled with a saturated solution of Epsom salt as shown in the diagram. In caves, the material deposited is calcium carbonate, dissolved out by groundwater.

# What Determines How Big Crystals Will Get?

## EXPERIMENT/DEMONSTRATION #105

### MATERIALS NEEDED:

Aluminum pan    Saturated salt water    Eyedropper    Glass jar    Candle
*Adult supervision and safety goggles are recommended.*

### PROCEDURE:

**Step 1:** Place an aluminum pan on top of a glass jar and place a candle at one outside edge of the pan.

**Step 2:** Place 12 drops of saturated salt water straight across the pan about a finger's width apart.

**Step 3:** Have your teacher light the candle. The burning candle should touch the bottom of the pan at one end of the line of drops.

**Step 4:** Observe the reaction for 25 minutes. At the end of that time, feel the crystal size of each of the droplets. Record your observations. Which crystals were the largest?

# How Can We Demonstrate Some of the Geological Features Formed by a Stream?

## EXPERIMENT/DEMONSTRATION #106

### MATERIALS NEEDED:

Soil tray
Water faucet
Soil
Clay
Sand
Gravel

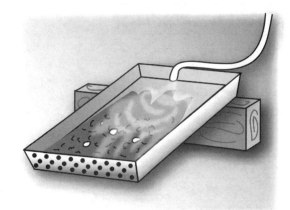

### PROCEDURE:

**Step 1:** A very effective working model that shows erosion, transportation, and the depositing of sediments can be set up easily. In a soil tray, place handfuls of soil, clay, sand, and gravel.

**Step 2:** Set the tray at a slight slope and run a rubber tube from the water faucet to the closed end of the tray to provide a constantly flowing stream. Make sure the soil tray is in a sink or a larger container to catch the water and soil that run off.

**Step 3:** By varying the rate of flow, the slope, and the materials in the tray, various geologic features can be produced in miniature.

**Record your observations:** _____

_____

_____

_____

_____

_____

_____

# How Can We Demonstrate the Action of Ice in Changing the Earth's Surface?

## EXPERIMENT/DEMONSTRATION #107

### MATERIALS NEEDED:

Baby food jar with lid
Grease pencil
Plastic resealable bag
Ruler

### PROCEDURE:

**Step 1:** Half-fill the baby food jar with water and put the lid on tightly. Mark the water line with the grease pencil and measure the height of the line from the bottom of the jar. Record this measurement.

**Step 2:** Put the jar inside the plastic bag and seal the bag. Carefully place the jar and bag in a freezer.

**Step 3:** Remove the jar from the freezer after the water has frozen. Mark the ice line. Measure and record the height of the ice line.

**Which line was higher?** _____

_____

**What will happen to rocks when water freezes in the cracks?**

_____

_____

_____

_____

_____

_____

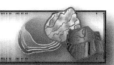

## How Can We Demonstrate the Action of Ice in Changing the Earth's Surface? (cont.)

## EXPERIMENT/DEMONSTRATION #108

### MATERIALS NEEDED:

Soil tray          Soil          Ice or ice cubes

### PROCEDURE:

**Step 1:** Set a soil tray in a sloping position and fill it with soil. Set up in a sink or larger container to catch any soil or water that runs off.

**Step 2:** Put some ice or ice cubes at the top of the incline and notice what happens as they melt.

**Step 3:** Pick up one of the ice cubes and rub it over the soil.

**What happens?** (Use the form at the beginning of this book or your own paper.)

## How Do We Know That Ice Contains Particles?

## EXPERIMENT/DEMONSTRATION #109

### MATERIALS NEEDED:

Icicle        White pan or white piece of paper

### PROCEDURE:

Let an icicle melt on a piece of white paper or in a white pan. Notice that it has picked up small particles from the roof. The sediment from the icicle may be thought of as a miniature glacial deposit.

## Additional Activity:
## Was This Area Covered by Glaciers?

Find out if the area in which you live was covered by glaciers. Locate evidence of glacial deposits, such as fields covered with stones and huge boulders in unusual places.

# How Are Kettle Holes Formed?

## EXPERIMENT/DEMONSTRATION #110

### MATERIALS NEEDED:

Pan     Soil     One or more ice cubes

Kettle holes are depressions where drainage water collects. Since there is no outlet to carry the water away, kettle holes often help maintain a relatively high water table over a wide area. They are believed to have been formed in glacial times by the melting of large blocks of ice beneath the surface when a glacier receded.

### PROCEDURE:

Place one or more ice cubes in a pan and cover with soil so the surface is level. When the ice melts, an excellent model of a kettle hole is formed.

# Does Air Carry Sediments?

## EXPERIMENT/DEMONSTRATION #111

### MATERIALS NEEDED:

White pan     Water

### PROCEDURE:

To show that air carries sediment, set a white pan filled with water out on the windowsill. After a day or two, observe the sediment that has collected in the pan.

# Additional Activity:
# What Does Wind Do to Debris on the Ground?

On a windy day, observe what the wind does to leaves, twigs, and other debris on the ground. Look in corners protected from the wind and notice that soil, leaves, and other materials are sometimes deposited there.

# *How Are Sand Dunes Formed?*

## *EXPERIMENT/DEMONSTRATION #112*

### MATERIALS NEEDED:

Dry sand or powdered soap        Pencil
Large box                        Electric fan
*Adult supervision is recommended.*

### PROCEDURE:

**Step 1:** Pour a pile of dry sand or powdered soap on the bottom of a large box cut away as shown in the diagram.

**Step 2:** Turn an electric fan on the pile and notice how the particles are moved. Notice that more particles are moved as the velocity of the wind increases.

**Step 3:** Put an obstacle such as a pencil or your finger in the path of the blowing sand or soap and relate this to snow fences and sand dunes.

## Additional Activity: What Makes Up Sand?

### MATERIALS NEEDED:

Coarse-grained sand       Sifting sieves of varying degrees
Hand lenses               Tweezers       Small condiment cups       Paper plates

### PROCEDURE:

Your teacher will give you a small cup of regular, coarse-grained sand. Try to think of creative ways to determine what the sand is made of. Devise some ways to sort the sand particles for identification. Then separate the different sand particles into small cups. Using field guides and reference materials, identify the particles that make up your sample of sand.

# What Are the Forces That Help Make Soil?

## EXPERIMENT/DEMONSTRATION #113

### MATERIALS NEEDED:

Class rock collection          Soil          Newspaper

### PROCEDURE:

Place one of the larger flat pieces of rock from the class' rock collection on a piece of newspaper and rub a smaller rock over it. Continue rubbing until some rock dust is worn from the rock. Examine the dust and compare it to soil.

The activities of animals, the action of freezing and thawing, the force of gravity, the work of streams, and many other factors are continually rubbing rocks together and wearing them away. With the aid of plants, the dust that is worn from rocks may eventually become good soil.

Grass fires, forest fires, and wasteful farming practices remove the cover of vegetation and allow the soil to erode. It takes many years to form good soil, so conserving soil is very important.

## Mohs Hardness Scale

Hardness is a property of minerals. Only about 12 of the 4,000 known minerals make up what are known as the rock-forming minerals. Minerals (and rocks) can be identified by their hardness. The hardness of a mineral can be determined by rubbing an unknown mineral against a known mineral or another object for which the hardness is known.

| Hardness | Mineral |
|---|---|
| 1 | Talc (easily scratched by your fingernail) |
| 2 | Gypsum (can be scratched by your fingernail, 2.5) |
| 3 | Calcite (barely can be scratched by a penny, 3) |
| 4 | Fluorite (easily scratched with a steel file or piece of glass, 5) |
| 5 | Apatite (can be scratched with a steel file or a piece of glass, 5) |
| 6 | Orthoclase (can scratch glass with difficulty) |
| 7 | Quartz (easily scratches both a steel file and glass) |
| 8 | Topaz (scratches quartz) |
| 9 | Corundum (scratches topaz) |
| 10 | Diamond (scratches everything else) |

# What Are the Constituencies of Soil?

## EXPERIMENT/DEMONSTRATION #114

### MATERIALS NEEDED:

Soil          Water
Tall glass jar or bottle (with lid)

### PROCEDURE:

**Step 1:** Put a handful of soil into a tall glass jar or bottle with water and stir the soil and water thoroughly.

**Step 2:** Shake the bottle or jar vigorously until both soil and water are thoroughly mixed. Put the jar or bottle where it will not be disturbed.

The next day, three layers or kinds of materials will be visible:

   a. Bottom layer: sand—the heaviest material, consisting of tiny bits of rocks.
   b. Second layer: clay or ground-up rock particles
   c. Top layer: decayed plant and animal material

## Additional Activity: What Are the Layers of Soil?

Visit a steep hillside and measure the depth of topsoil at the top and bottom of the slope. Dig holes about the size of post-holes to find the dividing line between topsoil and subsoil. Be sure to replace the soil that has been removed.

# How Is Soil Tested?

## EXPERIMENT/DEMONSTRATION #115

### MATERIALS NEEDED:

Soil-testing kit, if available  <u>OR</u>
Soil sample      Water      Flask      Litmus or pH paper

### PROCEDURE:

#### With a soil-testing kit:

Follow the directions included with the kit and discuss the importance of maintaining correct soil conditions for various crops. Point out reasons why some soils become too acidic and explain why lime is used to neutralize the acid.

#### Without a soil-testing kit:

**Step 1:**  Add a sample of soil to some water in a flask.

**Step 2:**  Allow the mixture to settle until there is a layer of clear water at the top. This water will contain dissolved matter and can be tested with litmus or pH paper. Mark the level of pH on the chart below.

### pH Levels

Depending on the method used, you may be able to pinpoint the pH level, or you may just be able to tell if the soil is acidic, neutral, or basic.

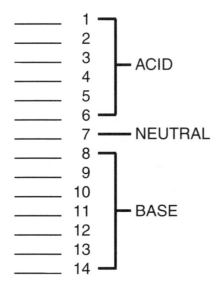

# How Is Soil Tested? (cont.)

## EXPERIMENT/DEMONSTRATION #116

### MATERIALS NEEDED:

Soil samples from different areas        Paper cups
Red and blue litmus paper        Marker        Water

### PROCEDURE:

**Step 1:** Place some soil from each sample in paper cups and label them with a marker, denoting the areas from which they came. Add enough water to make the soil fairly moist.

**Step 2:** Place a piece of red and a piece of blue litmus paper in each cup.

**Step 3:** After five minutes, remove the litmus papers from each cup and place them in front of their respective cups.

**What types of soil have been tested?** _____

_____

_____

_____

- If blue litmus paper turns red, the soil is acidic in nature.
- If red litmus paper turns blue, the soil is base or alkali in nature.
- If there is no change in color to the paper, the soil is neither an acid nor a base.

# How Can We Demonstrate Soil Erosion and Conservation?

## EXPERIMENT/DEMONSTRATION #117

### MATERIALS NEEDED:

Two wood or plastic trays (not less than two feet by six inches and closed at one end)
Funnels, bottles, buckets        Watering can or a coffee can with holes in the bottom
Wire mesh or screen              Tacks or small nails            Soil          Sod

A pair of wooden or plastic troughs or trays similar to those in the diagram represent a very effective device for conducting various soil erosion and conservation experiments. Such troughs can be made quickly in the woodshop or even in the classroom. For best results, the troughs should not be less than two feet in length and six inches in width, and should be closed at one end. A little caulking around the inside corners will make them watertight. (This is not necessary if plastic trays are used.)

Pieces of wire mesh or screen should be tacked over the open ends of the troughs as shown. Large funnels and plastic bottles and ordinary buckets can be used to catch the overflow water.

On practically every school campus, a suitable place can be found for carrying out conservation experiments and demonstrations outdoors. The following experiments can, however, be conducted indoors as well.

### PROCEDURE:

**#1:** Fill one tray with loose soil and the other with firmly packed soil. With both trays tilted slightly, water each equally with a watering can or a coffee can with holes punched in the bottom. Which tray loses more soil?

**#2:** Fill both trays with soil, but cover one with sod. Water both trays equally. Which tray loses more soil?

**#3:** Fill both trays with soil, but give one more slope than the other. Water both trays equally. Which tray loses more soil?

Possibilities for additional experiments are obvious and are often suggested by students.

# How Is the Earth's Surface Built Up?

## EXPERIMENT/DEMONSTRATION #118

### MATERIALS NEEDED:

Several thin sheets of colored Plasticine     Knife

### PROCEDURE:

**Step 1:** To show what happens to horizontal strata of sedimentary rock when they are compressed laterally, stack several thin sheets of colored Plasticine on top of each other.

**Step 2:** Place a hand near each end of the stack and push toward the middle. The stacked materials form a hump, or mountain.

**Step 3:** Slice the ridges crosswise with a knife to show the curved rock layers (synclines and anticlines).

# How Can We Show a Cause for Faulting?

## EXPERIMENT/DEMONSTRATION #119

### MATERIALS NEEDED:

Two books the same size      Pan of water      Pan of sand
Platform balance             Teaspoon

### PROCEDURE:

**Step 1:** To show how accumulated sediments may cause faulting, balance two books close together on the two arms of a platform balance. The pages of the books will represent rock layers.

**Step 2:** On top of one book, set a pan of sand to represent a mountain. On top of the other book, set a pan of water to represent an ocean.

**Step 3:** Point out that as the mountain erodes, sediments are carried into the ocean. To represent this, take a teaspoonful of sand from the mountain and dump it into the ocean. This disturbs the balance of the earth's crust and causes a fault (earthquake).

# What Is the Cause of
# Unequal Heating of the Land?

## EXPERIMENT/DEMONSTRATION #120

### MATERIALS NEEDED:

Soil
Two beakers
Two thermometers
Water
Support (ring stand)

### PROCEDURE:

**Step 1:** Place some soil in one beaker and fill the other beaker with water to the same level. Support a thermometer in each beaker with the bulb just covered as shown in the diagram.

**Step 2:** Allow the containers to remain in a shaded place until their temperatures are the same.

**Step 3:** Set the beakers in direct sunlight.

**Step 4:** Record the thermometer readings every ten minutes.

*Which beaker gains heat faster?* _____

*Why?* _____

_____

_____

# What Is the Cause of Unequal Heating of the Land? (cont.)

## EXPERIMENT/DEMONSTRATION #121

### MATERIALS NEEDED:

Three similar tin cans
Three thermometers
Black paint
White paint
Water
Electric heater
*Adult supervision and the use of safety goggles are recommended.*

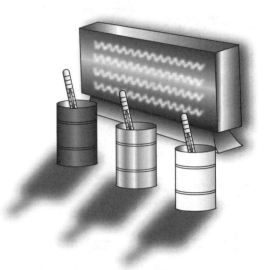

### PROCEDURE:

Show how the absorption of radiation varies with the color and nature of the surface on which solar energy falls.

**Step 1:** Obtain three similar tin cans; paint one black, paint one white, and leave the third unpainted.

**Step 2:** Put an equal amount of water and a thermometer in each can.

**Step 3:** Set the cans at equal distances from an electric heater.

**Step 4:** Prepare a table for data and record the temperature of the water in each can at five-minute intervals.

**What happens to the water in each can?** _____

_____

**Why?** _____

_____

_____

# What Is the Cause of Unequal Heating of the Land? (cont.)

## EXPERIMENT/DEMONSTRATION #122

### MATERIALS NEEDED:

Two test tubes
Two thermometers
Test tube rack
Black marker
Water

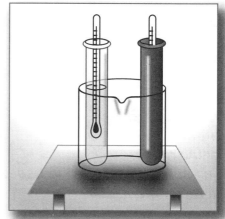

### PROCEDURE:

**Step 1:** Pour equal amounts of water into two test tubes, one of which is covered with black marker.

**Step 2:** Insert thermometers in each and set the two test tubes side by side in a test tube rack in direct sunlight.

**What happens?** _____
_____
_____

**Why?** _____
_____
_____

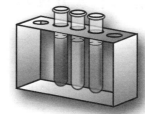

# Is Water a Poor Conductor of Heat?

## EXPERIMENT/DEMONSTRATION #123

### MATERIALS NEEDED:

Test tube (labeled "A" on top and "B" on bottom)
Water                              Bunsen burner
Apparatus to hold test tube in an inclined position
*Adult supervision and the use of safety goggles are recommended.*

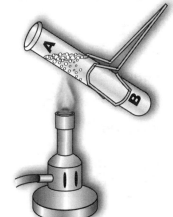

### PROCEDURE:

**Step 1:** Fill a test tube with cold water.

**Step 2:** Incline the test tube and heat the top region.

**What happens to region "A" (top)?** _____

_____

**What happens to region "B" (bottom)?** _____

_____

**What does this experiment tell us about the conducting ability of**

**water and glass?** _____

_____

_____

# Is Water a Poor Conductor of Heat? (cont.)

## EXPERIMENT/DEMONSTRATION #124

### MATERIALS NEEDED:

Test tube                Tongs to hold test tube

Ice cube                 Bunsen burner

Length of solder wire, coiled to fit inside the test tube

*Adult supervision and the use of safety goggles are recommended.*

### PROCEDURE:

**Step 1:** Hold a piece of ice in the bottom of a tilted test tube with a coil of solder wire.

**Step 2:** Heat the upper part of the test tube.

**What happens to the ice?** _____

_____

_____

**What happens to the wire?** _____

_____

_____

**What happens to the test tube?** _____

_____

_____

# How Many Inches of Snow Equal One Inch of Rain?

## EXPERIMENT/DEMONSTRATION #125

### MATERIALS NEEDED:

Snow
Ruler
Two matching juice cans

### PROCEDURE:

**Step 1:** Obtain a column of snow from a recent snowfall. Measure the height of the column of snow in the juice can and then melt it in the other can.

**Step 2:** Measure the depth of water and determine the difference.

**Step 3:** Repeat with different types of snow (e.g., dry, flaky snow or wet, heavy snow).

# How Can We Demonstrate Dew?

## EXPERIMENT/DEMONSTRATION #126

### MATERIALS NEEDED:

Ice
Water
Tin can or glass
Thermometer

### PROCEDURE:

**Step 1:** Put some ice and water into a tin can or glass. Place a thermometer in the can or glass. (Do not stir the mixture with the thermometer.)

**Step 2:** Observe the setup and notice the drops of water on the outside of the can or glass.

**Step 3:** At the second the water droplets form, measure the temperature of the ice/water mixture. This temperature is the dew point. Dew is formed by some of the water vapor in the air changing to drops of water by cooling, such as on the tin can or glass.

# How Can We Make Frost?

## EXPERIMENT/DEMONSTRATION #127

### MATERIALS NEEDED:

Wet paper towel or cloth
Large, deep beaker with cover
Can
Crushed ice
Salt

### PROCEDURE:

**Step 1:** Place a wet paper towel or cloth in a large covered beaker to raise the humidity.

**Step 2:** Set a can containing a mixture of crushed ice and salt in the beaker and cover it again. A thick layer of frost should form.

**Step 3:** Compare the conditions within the beaker with those under which natural frost forms.

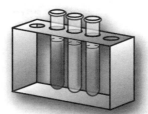

# How Can We Make a Simple Rain Gauge?

## EXPERIMENT/DEMONSTRATION #128

### MATERIALS NEEDED:

Large plastic bottle
Marker or tape
Marbles or rocks
Ruler
Water
Scissors or knife
*Adult supervision is recommended.*

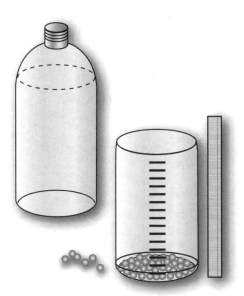

### PROCEDURE:

**Step 1:** If needed, ask an adult to help cut a large plastic bottle as seen in the diagram. Place thin strips of tape or marker on the bottle 10 millimeters apart.

**Step 2:** Place marbles or rocks in the bottom of the bottle for weight to stabilize the gauge.

**Step 3:** Pour water into the gauge up to the first mark or piece of tape.

**Step 4:** Record rainfall daily (each mark is 10 milliliters of rainfall).

**Step 5:** Empty the bottle at the end of each day.

# *Glossary*

**absorption:** taken in; sucked up

**ailerons:** a pilot-controlled airfoil attached to, in, or near the trailing edge of an airplane wing

**air:** the elastic invisible mixture of gases (chiefly nitrogen and oxygen, as well as hydrogen, carbon dioxide, argon, neon, helium, etc.) that surrounds the earth

**air currents:** a vertical movement of air

**airplane:** a fixed-wing aircraft, heavier than air, that is kept aloft by the aerodynamic forces of air as it is driven forward by a screw propeller or be other means, such as jet propulsion

**altostratus:** the type of gray or bluish cloud found at intermediate altitudes and consisting of a thick, dense, extensive layer of ice crystals and water droplets

**alum:** a double sulfate of a monovalent metal or radical with a trivalent metal; used as an astringent, as an emetic, and in the manufacture of baking powders, dyes, and paper

**anemometer:** a gauge for determining the force or speed of the wind and sometimes its direction

**anticline:** a sharply arched fold of stratified rock from whose central axis the strata slope downward in opposite directions

**apparatus:** the instruments, materials, tools, etc., needed for a specific use

**aquarium:** a tank, usually with glass sides, or a pool or bowl, etc., for keeping live water animals and water plants

**artesian well:** a well drilled deep enough to reach water that is draining down from higher surrounding ground above the well so that the pressure will force a flow of water upward

**artificial satellite:** man-made object put into orbit around a planet or moon

**atmosphere:** the gaseous envelope (air) surround the earth to a height of 621 miles

**atmospheric pressure:** the pressure due to the weight of the earth's atmosphere; one standard atmosphere equals 14.69 pounds per square inch of pressure and measures 29.92 inches in a barometer of mercury

**balancing point:** the point at which an object's weight is divided equally

**barometer:** an instrument for measuring atmospheric pressure, especially an aneroid barometer or an evacuated and graduated glass tube (mercury barometer); barometers are used in forecasting changes in the weather or finding height above sea level

**barometric pressure:** the pressure of the atmosphere as indicated by a barometer

**beaker:** a jarlike container of glass or metal with a lip for pouring, used by chemists

**bimetal (bimetallic):** of, containing, or using two metals, often two metals bonded together

**bimetal thermal strip:** two metals bonded together, usually brass and steel, with different heat expansion rates

**blotting paper:** a thick absorbent paper used to dry a surface that has just been written on with ink

**bulb:** the temperature-sensitive spherical tip of a thermometer

**Bunsen burner:** a small gas burner that produces a hot, blue flame, used in science laboratories; it consists of a hollow metal tube with holes at the bottom for admitting air to be mixed with gas

**calibrate:** to fix, correct, or check the graduations of (a measuring instrument, as a thermometer)

**capillary action:** upper movement of liquid through soil

**centrifugal force:** an apparent force tending to pull a thing outward when it is rotating around a center

**circumference:** the line bounding a circle, a rounded surface, or an area suggesting a circle

**cirrocumulus:** the type of white cloud resembling a small puff, flake, or streak, found at high altitudes and consisting of ice crystals and water droplets; mackerel sky

**cirrostratus:** the type of thin, whitish clouds; such clouds often produce the halo phenomenon

**cirrus:** the type of cloud resembling a wispy filament, found at high altitudes and consisting of ice crystals

**cloud:** a visible mass of tiny, condensed water droplets or ice crystals suspended in the atmosphere

**coagulate:** to cause to curdle; to cause (a liquid) to become a soft, semisolid mass

**compass:** any of various instruments for showing direction, especially one consisting of a magnetic needle swinging freely on a pivot and pointing to magnetic north

**condensation:** the act of condensing, as the reduction of a gas to a liquid

**conductor:** a substance or thing that is a channel of heat, electricity, sound, etc.

**conservation:** the act or practice of protecting from loss, waste, etc.; preservation

**contraction:** reduction in size, drawn together, narrow, shorten

**convection current:** the transfer of heat by means of current

**convex surface:** curved outward like the surface of a sphere

**copper shot:** small pellets made of copper

**crystal:** a clear transparent quartz; a solid that has a regularly repeating arrangement of its atoms

**cumulonimbus:** the type of dense cloud developing vertically through all cloud levels, consisting of water droplets, ice crystals, and sometimes hail, and associated with thunder, lightning, and heavy showers

**cumulus:** the type of bright, billowy cloud developing vertically through all cloud levels, with a dark, flat base, and consisting mostly of water droplets

**debris:** rough broken bits and pieces of stone, wood, glass, etc.

**delta:** a deposit of sand and soil, usually triangular, formed at the mouth of a river

**dew:** the condensation formed, usually during the night, on lawns, cars, etc., as a result of warm air contacting a cool surface

**distill:** to purify or refine

**drag:** a resisting force exerted on an aircraft parallel to its airstream and opposite in direction to its motion

**dry ice:** carbon dioxide solidified and compressed into snowlike cakes that vaporize at -78.5°C without passing through a liquid state; used as a refrigerant

**(sand) dune:** a rounded hill or ridge of sand heaped up by the action of the wind

**egg timer:** a device for measuring time

**electric charge:** as one body gains positive charge, some other body gains the same amount of negative charge; charges may be produced by rubbing together a variety of materials

**electrophorus:** an apparatus consisting of an insulated resin disc and a metal plate, used in generating static electricity by induction

**elevators:** a pilot-controlled airfoil attached to the trailing edge of the tail section's horizontal stabilizers to make an aircraft go up or down and to control pitching

**emulsion:** a stable colloidal suspension, consisting of an immiscible liquid dispersed and held in another liquid by substances called emulsifiers

**Epsom salt:** a white crystalline salt, used as a cathartic

**erosion:** wearing away by wind or water; disintegrating

**escapement:** the part in a mechanical clock or watch that controls the speed and regularity of the balance wheel or pendulum, and thereby of the entire mechanism, by the movement of a notched wheel, one tooth of which is permitted to escape from the detaining catch at a time

**evaporating dish:** open dish with liquid

**evaporation:** to change a liquid or a solid into vapor; drive out or draw off in the form of vapor

**exhaust:** to draw off or let out completely (air, gas, etc.), as from a container, or to use up; to expend completely

**expansion:** enlargement, dilation

**expansion ball and ring:** brass ring and ball that may be heated and cooled to show expansion and contraction

**fault:** a fracture or zone of fractures in rock strata together with movement that displaces the sides relative to one another

**filter:** device for separating solid particles, impurities, etc., from a liquid or gas by passing it through a porous substance

**flask:** any small bottle-shaped container with a narrow neck, used in laboratories, etc.

**fossil:** any hardened remains or imprints of plant or animal life of some previous geologic period, preserved in the earth's crust, including petrified wood, resin, etc.

**frost:** the ice crystals that form directly on freezing surfaces as contacted by moist air

**funnel:** an instrument consisting of an inverted cone with a hole at the small end, or a tapering or cylindrical tube with a wide, cone-shaped mouth, for pouring liquids and powders into containers with small openings

**galvanized:** to plate metal with zinc, originally by applying electric current

**gas:** the lightest form of a substance in which it can expand indefinitely to fill its container; form that is neither liquid nor solid

**gauge:** any device for measuring something, as the thickness of wire, the amount of liquid in a container, steam pressure, etc.

**glacial deposit:** rocks or soil left after a glacier melts or recedes

**glacier:** a large mass of ice and snow that forms in areas where the rate of snowfall contantly exceeds the rate at which the snow melts; it moves slowly outward from the center of accumulation or down a mountain until it melts or breaks away

**graduated cylinder:** a cylinder, generally glass, calibrated for measuring

**granite:** a very hard, crystalline, plutonic rock, gray to pink in color, consisting of feldspar, quartz, and smaller amounts of other minerals

**gravel:** loose mixture of pebble and rock fragments coarser than sand, often mixed with clay

**hairspring:** very slender, hairlike coil that controls the regular movement of the balance wheel in a watch or clock

**helicopter:** a kind of vertical-lift aircraft, capable of hovering or moving in any direction, having a motor-driven, horizontal rotor

**hot plate:** a small, portable device for cooking food or heating something, usually with only one or two gas or electric burners

**hourglass:** an instrument for measuring time by the trickling of sand, mercury, water, etc. through a small opening from one glass bulb to another below it, in a fixed period of time, especially one hour

**humidity:** moistness, dampness, the amount or degree of moisture in the air

**hygrometer:** any of various instruments for measuring the absolute or relative amount of moisture in the air

**hypothesis:** an unproved theory, proposition, supposition, etc., tentatively accepted to explain certain facts or (working hypothesis) to provide a basis for further investigation, argument, etc.

**igneous:** formed by volcanic action or intense heat, as rocks solidified

from molten magma at or below the surface of the earth

**jet:** an airplane propelled by jet propulsion, forcing gas out in a stream

**jet propulsion:** a method of propelling airplanes, boats, etc., that uses the reaction force created when compressed outside air and hot exhaust gases are forced through a jet nozzle

**kettle hole:** a depression in a glacial drift remaining after the melting of an isolated mass of buried ice

**lamp wick:** a piece of cord, tape, or bundle of threads designed to absorb fuel by capillary action

**lath:** any of the thin narrow strips of wood used in lattices or nailed to two-by-fours, rafters, etc.

**latitude:** angular distance measured in degrees north or south from the equator

**lift pump:** a suction pump that raises a column of liquid to the level of a spout, out which the liquid runs of its own accord

**limestone:** rock consisting mainly of calcium carbonate, often composed of the organic remains of sea animals, as mollusks, corals, etc., used as a building stone, a source of lime, etc.; when crystallized by heat and pressure, it becomes marble

**liquid:** readily flowing; fluid; having its molecules moving freely with respect to each other so as to flow readily, unlike a solid, but because of the cohesive forces not expanding indefinitely like a gas

**litmus paper:** absorbent paper treated with litmus, used as an acid-base indicator

**loam:** a rich soil composed of clay, sand, and some organic matter

**longitude:** distance east or west on the earth's surface, measured as

an arc of the equator between the meridian, usually the one passing through Greenwich, England

**manometer:** an instrument for measuring the pressure of gases or liquids

**map:** a drawing or other representation, usually on a flat surface, of all or part of the earth's surface, ordinarily showing countries, bodies of water, cities, mountains, etc.

**meridian:** a great circle of the earth passing through the geographical poles and any given point on the surface

**metamorphic:** of, characterized by, or caused from a change of form, shape, structure, or substance; a type of rock formed by the transformation of pre-existing rocks

**mineral:** an inorganic substance occurring naturally in the earth and having a consistent and distinctive set of physical properties and a composition that can be expressed by a chemical formula

**moisture:** water or other liquid causing a slight wetness or dampness

**nimbostratus:** the type of extensive gray cloud that obscures the sun, found at low altitudes and consisting of dense, dark layers of water droplets, rain, or snow

**orbit:** the actual or imaginary path taken by a celestial body during its periodic revolution around another body

**oxbow lake:** sharp bend in a river that has been dammed at both ends forming a lake

**parachute:** a cloth device usually shaped like an umbrella when expanded, and used to slow the falling speed of a person or thing dropping from an airplane, etc.

**paraffin:** a white, waxy, odorless, tasteless solid substance consisting of a mixture of straight-chain, saturated hydrocarbons

**pendulum:** an object hung from a fixed point so as to swing freely back and forth under the combined forces of gravity and momentum; often used in regulating the movement of clocks

**permeability:** the state or quality of being open to passage or penetration

**pH:** a symbol for the degree of acidity or alkalinity of a solution

**pith ball:** soft, spongy material, usually from a plant, formed into a ball; very sensitive to electrical charge

**place:** a particular area or locality; region

**plasticene:** an oil-based modeling paste, used as a substitute for clay or wax

**porous:** full of pores, through which fluids, air, or light may pass

**precipitation:** a depositing of rain, snow, sleet, etc.

**propeller:** a device on a ship or aircraft consisting typically of two or more blades twisted to describe a helical path as they rotate with the hub on which they are mounted, and serving to propel the craft by the backward thrust of air or water

**radiation:** the process in which energy in the form of rays of light, heat, etc., is sent out through space from atoms and molecules as they go through internal changes

**radius:** any straight line extending from the center to the periphery (outside) of a circle or sphere

**rate:** the amount, degree, etc., of anything in relation to units of something else (rate of speed per hour)

**relative humidity:** the amount of moisture in the air as compared with the maximum amount that the air could contain at the same temperature, expressed as a percentage

**reservoirs:** places where anything is collected and stored, generally in large quantities; especially a natural or artificial lake or pond in which water is collected and stored for use

**ring stand:** metal upright for clamping scientific equipment in some science experiments

**rock:** mineral matter variously composed, formed in masses or large quantities in the earth's crust by the action of heat, water, etc.

**rocket:** any of various devices, typically cylindrical, containing liquid or solid propellants, which when ignited produce hot gases or ions that escape through a rear vent and drive the container forward by the principle of reaction

**rubber tubing:** a slender pipe made of rubber used for conveying fluids

**rudder:** broad flat movable piece of wood or metal hinged vertically at the stern of a boat or ship, used for steering

**runoff:** something that runs off, as rain in excess of the amount absorbed by the ground

**sandstone:** a common bedded sedimentary rock much used for building, composed largely of sand grains, mainly quartz, held together by silica lime, etc.

**satellite:** a moon traveling around a larger planet; a man-made object rocketed into orbit around Earth, the moon, etc.

**saturated:** filled to capacity; having absorbed all that can be taken up

**sealing wax:** combination of resin and turpentine used for sealing letters, dry cells, etc.; it is hard at normal temperature, but softens when heated

**sediment:** matter that settles to the bottom of a liquid; matter deposited by water or wind

**sedimentary:** containing sediment; rock formed by the deposit of sediment

**seed:** in a cloud it provides a partial nucleus around which water vapor forms

**sextant:** an instrument used by navigators for measuring the angular distance of the sun, a star, etc., from the horizon as in finding the position of a ship

**shale:** a kind of fine-grained, thinly bedded sedimentary rock formed largely by the hardening of clay; it splits easily into thin layers

**shallow:** not deep

**siphon:** bent tube used for carrying liquid from a reservoir over the top of the edge of its container to a point below the surface of the reservoir; the tube must be filled, as by suction, before flow will start

**slate:** a hard, fine-grained, metamorphic rock that cleaves naturally into thin, smooth-surfaced layers

**smoke paper:** burned paper still emitting smoke

**soil:** the surface layer of the earth, supporting plant life

**solder wire:** a metal alloy used when melted for joining or patching metal parts or surfaces

**solid:** tending to keep its form rather than to flow or spread out like a liquid or gas; relatively firm or compact

**stalactite:** an icicle-shaped, secondary mineral deposit that hangs from the roof in a cave and is formed by the evapoation of water that is full of minerals

**stalagmite:** a cone-shaped, secondary mineral deposit built up on the floor of a cave by dripping minerals

**stratocumulus:** the type of white or gray cloud found at low altitudes and consisting of large, smooth or patchy layers of water droplest and possibly some hail or snow

**stratum:** a horizontal layer or section of material, especially any of several lying one upon another

**stratus:** type of gray cloud found at low altitudes and consisting of a uniform layer of water droplets and sometimes ice crystals

**supersaturated:** to make more highly concentrated than in normal saturation at a given temperature

**synclines:** a down fold in stratified rocks from whose central axis the beds rise upward and outward in opposite directions

**temperature:** the degree of hotness or coldness of anything, usually as measured on a thermometer

**terrarium:** an enclosure, such as a glass tank, in which to keep small land animals and plants

**test tube:** a tube of thin, transparent glass closed at one end, used in chemical experiments, etc.

**thermal:** having to do with heat

**thermometer:** an instrument for measuring temperatures, consisting of a graduated glass tube with a sealed, capillary bore in which mercury, colored alcohol, etc., rises or falls as it expands or contracts from changes in temperature

**thermostat:** an apparatus for regulating temperature, especially one that automatically controls a heating or cooling unit

**thistle tube:** a thistle-shaped glass tube used to move liquids in science experiments; has various uses

**thrust:** to push with sudden force; drive

**time:** indefinite, unlimited duration in which things are considered as happening in the past, present, or future

**time cone:** calibrated cone placed over a globe at the North Pole showing the time zones

**tongs:** a device for seizing or lifting objects, having two long arms pivoted or hinged together

**topsoil:** the upper layer of soil, usually darker and richer than the subsoil; surface soil

**tumbler:** an ordinary drinking glass without foot or stem

**vacuum pump:** pump used to draw air out of a sealed space

**vessel:** a utensil for holding something, as a vase, bowl, pot, kettle, etc.

**water table:** the level below which the ground is saturated with water

**water vapor:** water in the form of gas; steam

**weather:** general condition of the atmosphere at a particular time and place, with regard to the temperature, moisture, cloudiness, and so on

**weather vane:** an instrument that swings in the wind to show the direction from which the wind is blowing

**wind:** air in motion; specifically any noticeable natural movement of air parallel to the earth's surface

# Answer Keys

**Experiment/Demonstration #1 (p. 1)**
The egg will drop into the bottle in a matter of seconds. The flame "uses up" most of the oxygen in the milk bottle. Since there is then less pressure pushing upward and more pressure pushing downward, the egg is literally "pushed" into the bottle.

**Experiment/Demonstration #2 (p. 2)**
Atmospheric pressure will collapse the can.

**Experiment/Demonstration #3 (p. 2)**
The water does not run out of the glass because of the atmospheric pressure on the surface of the water in the vessel.

**Experiment/Demonstration #4 (p. 3)**
Atmospheric pressure will collapse the can since the pressure is greater on the outside of the can.

**Experiment/Demonstration #5 (p. 4)**
The card will "stick" to the top of the glass. The upward push of the air kept the card and water in place. Simply stated, the water "drove" most of the air out of the glass. The force pressing against the card was greater—had more strength—than the air pressure contained in the water-filled glass.

**Experiment/Demonstration #6 (p. 5)**
Water will stop flowing from the hole. Lift your hand and water will start to flow again.

**Experiment/Demonstration #7 (p. 6)**
You won't be able to drink because of the lack of air pressure from outside the bottle.

**Experiment/Demonstration #8 (p. 7)**
When the stopper is loosened, it allows outside air pressure to enable you to drink water.

**Experiment/Demonstration #9 (p. 8)**
The pressure of the atmosphere on the surface of the water in the dish keeps the water from running out of the jar.

**Experiment/Demonstration #13 (p. 12)**
When copper wire is heated, it will expand, causing the weight to slowly drop to the table and stop swinging freely. When the wire is cooled, it will contract to its original length.

**Experiment/Demonstration #14 (p. 13)**
Heat caused the wire to expand and drop the weight closer to the table. As the wire cooled, it contracted to its original length.

**Experiment/Demonstration #15 (p. 14)**
When heated, the strip will bend due to the unequal expansion of the two metals. Since the expansion of brass is greater than steel, brass is on the outside of the band.

**Experiment/Demonstration #17 (p. 16)**
When heated, copper wire expands more than tin; this causes one end to bend when the other end is clamped in a fixed position.

**Experiment/Demonstration #18 (p. 17)**
Heating expands the liquid, and it rises into the tube. Cooling contracts the liquid, causing its level to fall.

**Experiment/Demonstration #19 (p. 18)**
When one flask is heated, the air expands, driving some of the air out of the flask. The air in the heated flask will then weigh less than the air in the unheated flask, causing the two flasks to be unbalanced—the heated one moving up; the unheated moving down.

**Experiment/Demonstration #20 (p. 19)**
The heated air that is driven from the flask is pushed into the balloon, blowing up the balloon.

**Experiment/Demonstration #21 (p. 20)**
The coated tube has a higher temperature.

**Experiment/Demonstration #22 (p. 21)**
The colored water moves through the glass tube, showing convection currents.

**Experiment/Demonstration #23 (p. 22)**
The spiral rotates, showing convection currents of air.

**Experiment/Demonstration #25 (p. 23)**
The column rises when heated and falls when cooled.

**Experiment/Demonstration #29 (p. 27)**
As water evaporates from the cloth, it weighs less, upsetting the balance of the stick.

**Experiment/Demonstration #30 (p. 28)**
The water will evaporate more quickly from the vessel that has more surface area. The large surface area allows for more interaction between the water and air, causing more evaporation.

**Experiment/Demonstration #32 (p. 29)**
The alcohol evaporates. The temperature of the hand decreases.

**Experiment/Demonstration #34 (p. 31)**
The dew point is determined by the individual place where the experiment takes place—the temperature when dew is formed.

**Experiment/Demonstration #36 (p. 32)**
Fog forms in the bottle with hot water because of the meeting of the hot and cold air. There is no fog in the bottle with cold water because there is not enough temperature difference between the cold water and the ice cube.

**Experiment/Demonstration #40 (p. 36)**
Blowing in the jar raises relative humidity, and with the smoke inside, the conditions are perfect for condensation. When pressure is suddenly released, smog appears. When the jar is blown into again, the smog disappears, just as the smog will reappear if pressure is suddenly released again.

**Experiment/Demonstration #41 (p. 37)**
Raindrops freeze as they pass through cold layers of air in the container and in the air on the way to the earth.

**Experiment/Demonstration #42 (p. 38)**
The water pressure increases as the thistle tube goes deeper under water.

**Experiment/Demonstration #46 (p. 40)**
The looser the soil, the faster the water goes into the soil.

**Experiment/Demonstration #60 (p. 50)**
The moving air lessens air pressure as it rolls over the curved surface.

**Experiment/Demonstration #61 (p. 51)**
Lift occurs, and the platform balance becomes unbalanced because of the change in air pressure.

**Experiment/Demonstration #62 (p. 52)**
The air moves in one direction while the fan is moving in the opposite direction.

**Experiment/Demonstration #63 (p. 53)**
The paper sticks straight out because the fast air above is low pressure, and the slow high pressure air below keeps it straight out.

**Experiment/Demonstration #64 (p. 54)**
The flame goes toward the card because as the air goes around it, the air becomes turbulent, which slows and turns the flow.

**Experiment/Demonstration #65 (p. 55)**
Air currents move smoothly around the streamlined cardboard, pushing the flame outward.

**Experiment/Demonstration #68 (p. 56)**
The cork "pops" out of the bottle because the alcohol expands.

**Experiment/Demonstration #70 (p. 58)**
Gas forces the cork from the bottle. The gas and bottle go in different directions.

**Experiment/Demonstration #71 (p. 59)**
A jet of water through the tube shows thrust.

**Experiment/Demonstration #72 (p. 60)**
The can spins around as water comes out of the holes.

**Experiment/Demonstration #80 (p. 66)**
1. The pull on the cord represents gravity. The outward pull on the cord represents centrifugal force.
2. The moon continues to revolve about the earth because its own inertia keeps it in motion. The centrifugal force and gravity exactly balance each other.
3. The stopper moves more rapidly when the orbit is shortened. The nearer a satellite is to the earth, the greater the pull of gravity. Artificial satellites must travel with tremendous speed to have enough centrifugal force to balance the pull of gravity upon them.

**Experiment/Demonstration #92 (p. 75)**
The water becomes cloudy. The sharp edges have been rounded and worn away.

**Experiment/Demonstration #98 (p. 81)**
Roots of the bean seeds start to penetrate the plaster, causing the plaster to crack or scale off.

**Experiment/Demonstration #99 (p. 82)**
The unprotected soil is washed and splashed away, whereas the soil forms columns under the coins.

**Experiment/Demonstration #103 (p. 84)**
Erosion occurs differently in each metal pan, depending on the protection from rain.

**Additional Activity #3 (p. 85)**
The lighter and smaller pieces are suspended the longest, making them the easiest to get carried away.

**Additional Activity #5 (p. 85)**
As the drop height increases, the splatter size increases.

**Experiment/Demonstration #105 (p. 86)**
The drops farthest away from the flame form the largest crystals.

**Experiment/Demonstration #107 (p. 88)**
The ice line should be higher. Water expands as it freezes in cracks of rocks causing the rocks to break more.

**Experiment/Demonstration #108 (p. 89)**
Ice cubes pick up soil particles, and when they slide downhill and melt, the soil is deposited where they melt.

**Experiment/Demonstration #117 (p. 96)**
1. The tray with loose soil loses the most soil.
2. The tray without sod loses the most soil.
3. The tray with the most slope loses the most soil.

**Experiment/Demonstration #120 (p. 98)**
The beaker with soil heats faster. Soil heats and cools more rapidly than water.

**Experiment/Demonstration #121 (p. 99)**
Water in the white can should be the coolest, while the water in the black can should be the warmest. The white can reflects the heat, while the black can absorbs the heat.

**Experiment/Demonstration #122 (p. 100)**
The water in the test tube that has been colored should be the hotter. The black test tube absorbs more heat from the sun.

**Experiment/Demonstration #123 (p. 101)**
Region A will boil, but region B will remain cold. The test tube could be held with your hand in region B, while region A is boiling. This shows that both water and glass are poor conductors of heat.

**Experiment/Demonstration #124 (p. 102)**
The ice will melt slowly. The top part of the tube will gradually get hot. The wire could get warm depending on the amount of time to melt the size of the ice cube.

*Acknowledgement: The Illinois Department of Education*